a big little life

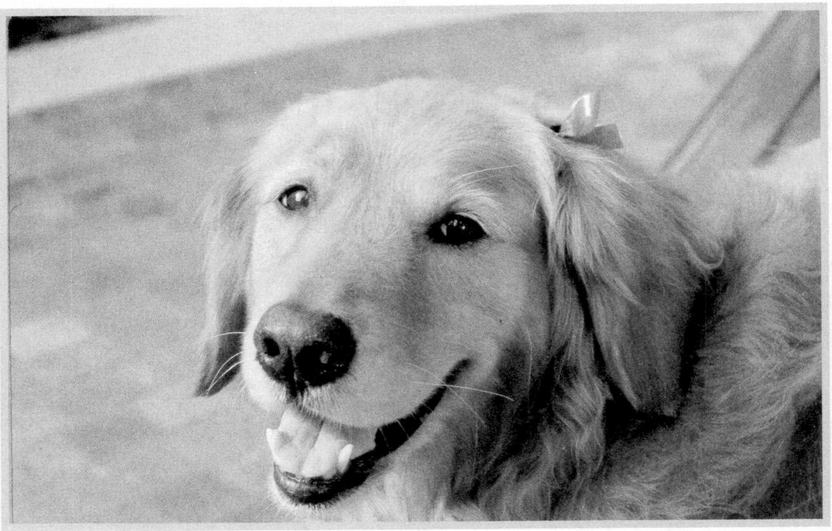

HYPERION

NEW YORK

a big little life

a memoir of a joyful dog

DEAN KOONTZ

Printed in the United States of America. For information address Hyperion, 114 Fifth Avenue, New York, NY 10011.

Library of Congress Cataloging-in-Publication Data is available upon request.

ISBN 978-1-4013-2352-3

Hyperion books are available for special promotions and premiums. For details contact the HarperCollins Special Markets Department in the New York office at 212-207-7528, fax 212-207-7222, or e-mail spsales@harpercollins.com.

Design by Chris Welch
Photographs by Monique Stauder

FIRST EDITION

10 9 8 7 6 5 4 3 2 1

SUSTAINABLE FORESTRY INITIATIVE
Certified Fiber Sourcing
www.sfiprogram.org

THIS LABEL APPLIES TO TEXT STOCK

We try to produce the most beautiful books possible, and we are also extremely concerned about the impact of our manufacturing process on the forests of the world and the environment as a whole. Accordingly, we've made sure that all of the paper we use has been certified as coming from forests that are managed to ensure the protection of the people and wildlife dependent upon them.

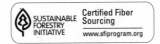

To Gerda, who shared the wonder
and the loss, who knows that the pain
was so great because the joy before
it was even greater, and who had the
courage to do it all again.
Bliss to you.

Dogs live most of life
in Quiet Heart.
Humans live mostly next door
in Desperate Heart.
Now and then will do you good
to live in our zip code.

—TRIXIE KOONTZ, *Bliss to You*

a big little life

1

a spooky moment around which the entire story revolves

THE SPOOKY MOMENT central to this story comes on an evening more than ten years ago.

Trixie, a three-year-old golden retriever of singular beauty and splendid form, adopted the previous September, is in her fourth month with my wife, Gerda, and me.

She is joyful, affectionate, comical, intelligent, remarkably well behaved. She is also more self-possessed and dignified than I had ever realized a dog could be.

Already and unexpectedly, she has changed me as a person and as a writer. I am only beginning to understand the nature of those changes and where they will lead me.

January 1999:

Our first house in Newport Beach, in the neighborhood known as Harbor Ridge, had an exceptionally long upstairs hallway, actually a gallery open to the foyer below. Because this hall was carpeted and thus provided good traction for paws and because nothing breakable stood along its walls, I often played there with Trixie on days when the weather turned foul and on cool winter evenings when the sun set early.

Initially, I tossed a ball and sometimes a Kong toy down the hall. The Kong was about six inches long, made of hard rubber with an inch-wide hole through the middle. You could stuff a mixture of peanut butter and kibble in the hole, to keep your dog occupied for an hour or longer. I tried this twice, but Trixie managed to extract the tasty mixture from the Kong in five minutes, which was less time than I took to prepare it.

One evening the rubber Kong bounced wildly and smashed into a small oil painting, splitting the canvas. The painting was very old, and it was one of Gerda's favorites.

When she noticed the damage a few days later, I fessed up at once: "The dog did it."

"Even standing on her hind feet," Gerda said, "the dog isn't tall enough to do it."

Confident that my logic was unassailable, I said, "The dog was here in the hall when the damage occurred. The Kong toy was here. The Kong belongs to the dog. The dog wanted to play. If the dog wasn't so cute, I wouldn't have wanted to play with her. Hall, dog, Kong, cute, play—the damage to the painting was inevitable."

"So you're saying the dog is responsible because she's cute."

I refused to allow my well-reasoned position to be nit-picked. I resorted to my backup explanation: "Besides, maybe she isn't tall enough, but she knows where we keep the stepstool."

So, because the dog had damaged the painting, in subsequent play sessions in the hall, we could not use the rubber Kong. Furthermore, I would not throw the tennis ball anymore, but would only roll it.

I explained the new rules to Trixie, whose expression was somber. "This is a valuable teaching moment," I concluded. "You see, I'm sure, that if you had gone to your mother immediately after you damaged the painting and had taken responsibility, you would not now have this blemish on your reputation."

Following the new rules, I always released the tennis ball with a snap of the wrist that gave it the velocity to roll the length of the hall. Trixie thundered after the ball, either snaring it near the end of its journey or snatching it out of the air if it ricocheted off the leg of a console and took flight. She returned it to me with dispatch, and at once I fired it off again. After twenty minutes, her flanks heaved, her tongue lolled, and though she still considered the tennis ball to be a priceless treasure, she was prepared to entrust it to me for a while.

Lying on the floor, facing each other, Trixie panted and I stroked her luxurious golden coat as she caught her breath.

From the week she came into our lives, Trixie and I had spent some time most days lying on the floor together. I found it relaxing for the obvious reason that a cuddle with a loving dog is always calming. I also found it strange, because she would stare into my eyes as long as I wanted to meet hers—ten minutes, twenty, thirty—and she would rarely be the first to look away.

These sessions were meditation but also communication, though I can't explain what she communicated other than love. I can say that I frequently saw in her eyes a yearning to make herself understood in a complex way that only speech could facilitate.

Staring into Trixie's eyes, I was sometimes silent but at other times talked to her about my day, my problems, my hopes, whatever came into my head. Those who love dogs know well this kind of rap. The dog does not react—and is not expected to react—to any of this, but listens and wonders. Dogs swim through a sea of human speech, listening attentively for words they recognize, patiently striving to interpret what we say, although most of it is and always will be incomprehensible to them. No human being would have such patience. Counting the many commands she had been taught when in training to be an assistance dog and all that she had learned on her own—cookie, chicken, walk, duck, stepstool, oil, painting, restoration, electromagnetism—her vocabulary was at least a hundred words. It would more than double over the years. This got me thinking. . . . The recognition that words have meaning, the desire to remember them, the intention to act on those that are understood—does all of this lead to the conclusion that the dog also yearns to speak?

On that January night, because Trixie had been an undiluted joy during the previous four months and had already been a force for positive change in me, I said, "You're not just a dog. You can't fool me. I know what you *really* are."

As if in response, she raised her head, eased back slightly, and regarded me with what might have been concern. Golden retrievers have versatile brow muscles that allow them a wide range of facial expressions. She never before responded to me in this fashion, and I was amused to interpret her look as meaning, *Uh-oh, somehow I've blown my cover.*

"You're really an angel," I continued.

To my surprise, she scrambled to her feet as if in alarm, ran down the hall, turned, and stared back at me. Muscles tensed, legs spread for maximum balance, head lifted, ears raised as much as a golden can raise them, she seemed to be waiting for what I might say next.

I'm seldom speechless. Trixie's behavior, which seemed to be a *reaction* to my words, as if she understood every one of them, raised the fine hairs on the nape of my neck and left me mute.

Intrigued, I got to my knees, wondering what she would do next, but she continued to watch me intently when I rose to my feet.

For a minute or two we studied each other from a distance of twenty feet, as though we both expected something of consequence to happen. Her tail did not wag. It wasn't lowered as it would have been if she had been the least fearful. It was a perfect plume, as still as if she had stepped outside of time, where nothing could move her or even one hair upon her, nothing except her own will.

"Trixie?" I finally asked, and when I spoke, she retreated another ten or fifteen feet and turned again to face me in the same expectant stance as before.

This was not a dog who wanted solitude or even distance. The closer she could be to us, the happier she appeared. When I was writing, she would sometimes slink under my desk and curl herself into the shape of an ottoman, and she sighed with pleasure when I rested my stockinged feet on her. With Gerda even more than with me, this sixty-plus-pound creature behaved like a lapdog, most content when embraced.

This was the first and last time she wanted distance from me. As we stared at each other, I began to realize that regardless of what Trixie's behavior implied, if it implied anything at all, I should not pursue this matter further if only because it disturbed her. Besides, I was dealing here with the ineffable, the pursuit of which offers endless frustration but no reward other than the thrill of the chase.

I sat on the hallway floor, my back to the wall, legs straight in front of me, and I closed my eyes. The nape of my neck tingled for a while, but when the fine hairs stopped quivering, Trixie returned to me. She snuggled against my side. Putting her head in my lap, she allowed me to rub gently behind her ears and stroke her face.

Later, I told Gerda about the incident, but of course she could make no more of it than I could. We don't have paranormal experiences or go to psychics. We don't even read our daily horoscopes.

I write fiction for a living. I could spin a score of intriguing scenarios out of this one spooky moment with Trixie, but none would be as strange as the truth, if it could be known in this instance. Truth is *always* stranger than fiction. We craft fiction to match our sense of how things ought to be, but truth cannot be crafted. Truth *is,* and truth has a way of astonishing us to our knees, reminding us that the universe does not exist to fulfill our expectations.

Because we are imperfect beings who are self-blinded to the truth of the world's stunning complexity, we shave reality into paper-thin theories and ideologies that we can easily grasp, and we call them truths. But the truth of a sea, in all its immensity, cannot be embodied in one tide-washed pebble.

When we write a novel, concoct a new political system, devise a theory to explain the workings of the human mind or the evolution of the universe—we are fictioneers, bleaching the rich narrative of reality into a pale story that we can better comprehend. We go wrong when we don't admit the unknowable complexity of reality, but we go dangerously wrong when we claim that one pale story—or an anthology of them—is truth. We arrive at the paleness to *avoid* consideration of the daunting truth in all its fierce color and infinite detail.

I can never know the truth of that spooky moment with Trixie, but what I do know is that throughout the years she was ours to cherish, she continually surprised us, as truth will. She made us laugh every day, and at times we wept in anguish because of her. She weighed only sixty-something pounds, I occasionally called her Short Stuff, and she lived less than twelve years. In this big world, she was a little thing, but in all the ways that mattered, including the effect she had on those who loved her, she lived a big life.

In each little life, we can see great truth and beauty, and in each little life we glimpse the way of all things in the universe. If we allow ourselves to be enchanted by the beauty of the ordinary, we begin to see that all things are extraordinary. If we allow ourselves to be humbled by what we do not and cannot know, in our humility we are exalted. If we allow ourselves to recognize the mystery and the wonder of existence, our fogged minds clear. Thinking clearly, we follow wonder to awe, and in a state of awe, we are as close to true wisdom as we will ever be.

Trixie was innocent and joyful, but also at times enigmatic and solemn. I learned as much from this good dog as from all my years in school.

II

life before trixie

WE WERE NOT fortunate enough to have always lived in Newport Beach, California, and I was not always the kind of person who blamed damaged paintings on the dog, largely because, until Trixie, I didn't have a dog to blame.

Growing up in Bedford, Pennsylvania, I lived with my mother and father in a cramped four-room house. My maternal grandfather built the place. I loved Grandpa

John, but in spite of his many talents, he was no more suited to a career in residential construction than I am qualified to perform open-heart surgery.

In the insistently moist cellar, a pair of lightbulbs were nestled deep in the pockets between ceiling joists, allowing us to brighten the darkness only to a sinister murk that did not disturb the colonies of scheming fungus in the corners. As a child, I half believed that the fungus possessed a malevolent consciousness and waited patiently for me to let down my guard.

After my ninth birthday, I shared furnace-tending duties. The iron beast stood opposite the coal-room door. Mornings, I shook the grate to drop the cinders and ashes into the collection bin, shoveled coal through the main door, and lighted tinder to encourage the coal to burn more quickly. On those evenings when I had no school the next day, I would bank the fire to ensure hot coals for the morning and to keep the house heated through the night.

Banking the fire always proved to be an act of folly. This was not a forced-air furnace. Heat rose through a large iron grate in the living-room floor and traveled upstairs so slowly that on a bitter winter morning, water left overnight in a glass had turned to ice.

We had no bathroom until I was twelve, just a showerhead that sprouted from one cellar wall, over a drain in the concrete floor. Solely to serve the shower and the washing machine, water was heated by a kerosene burner designed by a pyromaniac. A large glass jug of fuel had to be inverted to feed a ring wick by gravity drip. The contraption was shaky, and I expected a kerosene fireball to bloom through the house and turn us into human torches.

A vivid imagination is a blessing if you want to be a writer, but it is also a curse. Sometimes, in the coal room, I wondered if this would be the occasion when the shovel would turn up the pale hand of a corpse concealed under the anthracite. As he was always threatening violence, I had cast my father in the role of murderer.

I can say two positive things about the cellar. First, hot water could be drawn from a faucet, whereas at the kitchen sink only cold water could be had and only by using a hand-operated pump that tapped a well. Second, although acrawl with spiders, the cellar harbored fewer eight-legged stalkers than the outhouse.

When I was eleven, my mother received a modest sum from the settlement of my grandfather's estate, and she used it to provide the house with indoor plumbing: a small bathroom with hot and cold running water, and faucets in place of the hand-operated pump at the kitchen sink. She also replaced the tar-paper roof with asphalt shingles.

We felt as if we had moved into a palace. After all, we now had a shiny porcelain throne instead of a wooden bench with a hole in it and spiders lurking below.

Although we had few possessions, we were always in danger of losing everything we owned. Our perpetual dance with destitution resulted from my father's conviction that what he earned would be squandered if spent to pay bills and the mortgage, considering that poker or craps offered him the opportunity to quadruple his holdings in a single evening.

If the cards and the dice proved treacherous, he required the consolation of a saloon. Buying a round for the guys at the bar allowed him to pass for the man of means he dreamed of being.

When not in bars or games of chance, my father held forty-four jobs over thirty-five years, many of them in sales, primarily as an insurance agent. More than once he was fired because he punched out the boss—never a smart career move—or a fellow worker who offended him. Sometimes he quit because he felt unappreciated, and probably because the current enterprise included no one whom he wanted to punch, which made the workday boring.

Although my mother was slender, pretty, and goodhearted, my father chased other women. At least two were female wrestlers. In the 1950s, female wrestlers were as rare as armless banjo players, and they were not the bikinied beauties who began thrashing around in mud during the '70s. My father had affairs with female wrestlers who had bigger biceps and deeper voices than he did.

When our telephone rang after midnight, the caller always proved to be one barkeep or another, reporting that my father had passed out drunk and needed to be removed from the premises before closing time. If the saloon lay within a few miles of home, my mother and I would trek there on foot and load my father into his car.

On one occasion, a woman at the bar asked my mother if we could give her a ride home, as her date had walked out on her. This sturdy blonde had a perm so tight that her curls would have served as life-saving shock absorbers if anyone had hit her on the head with a sledgehammer.

I sensed that in fact my gentle mother regretted not having a sledgehammer close at hand, but I was too young to figure out that the blonde's date had not walked out on her but had *passed out,* that he was my old man. Enlightenment came the following evening when, lying in bed, I listened to my parents downstairs as they argued about the curly one.

As a consequence of post-midnight, father-salvaging expeditions and other mortifying experiences related to his behavior, I grew up in a state of embarrassment. Because my father's shortcomings were widely known, I cringed when asked if I was Ray Koontz's boy. Instead of answering directly, I said my mother was Florence Koontz, because no shame came with that association.

From the moment they saw me in the cradle, two of my aunts were convinced that I was no less of a good-for-nothing than my father. If they chanced upon me, a seven-year-old, lazing dreamily in the summer sun, their faces clouded and they declared solemnly, "Just like your father," as if other boys my age were earning their first hundred dollars at a lemonade stand or volunteering to empty bedpans in nursing homes.

My dad's lack of interest in me, his fits of rage and violence when drinking, his threats to kill himself—and us—the anguish and anxiety he caused my mother: None of that affected me as deeply as the embarrassment he brought upon us by public drunkenness, skirt-chasing, a tendency to brag extravagantly, and other behavior that made him a subject of gossip and scorn.

By high school, I was shy and insecure, and I compensated for my low self-esteem by being quick with a funny line and playing the class clown. Language skills were my shield and my sword.

In no aspect of my life did shyness manifest more than in my interactions with the opposite sex. If I asked a girl for a date and she turned me down, I never asked her again. She might decline with sincere regret, and it might turn out to be true that her mother was in the hospital and her father incapacitated by two broken legs and her beloved sister stuck in the twenty-third century after participating in a secret government time-travel experiment. However, I assumed that she looked at me, saw my father, and decided that setting her hair on fire would be wiser than accepting my invitation to the sock hop followed by milk shakes at Dairy Queen.

Then in my senior year, along came Gerda Cerra. I had been attracted to certain girls before, charmed by them, captivated, but I had not previously been enchanted. I had not before been smitten. In fact, I thought it was not possible to be smitten if you were born after 1890. Petite, graceful, beautiful, Gerda had a soft voice that made every word seem intimate and romantic. When she said, "Something is hanging from the end of your nose," my heart soared. Not least of all, her self-possession seemed otherworldly.

That I pursued her, shy as I was, all the way from a senior-year date to a marriage proposal is a testament to the impact that she had on me—especially considering that she turned me down four times.

In the first instance, upon hearing which evening I hoped to take her to a movie, she claimed to be working at the dry cleaner that night. Previously, if a girl in a full-body cast pled immobility as a reason for not accepting a date, I assumed the truth was that she found me repellent, and thereafter I avoided her. But a week later, I approached Gerda with a second invitation.

This time she informed me that, on the evening in question, she would be working at the movie theater, behind the refreshment counter. Here was a young woman who either redefined the meaning of industrious or could not remember the dry-cleaner lie that she had told me a week earlier.

After taking two weeks to restore my courage, I asked her for another date—only to learn she had a babysitting job that night. She seemed to be sincere, but everyone believed Hitler, too, when he claimed that he wouldn't invade Poland, and we know how that turned out. I did not think Gerda intended to invade Poland, and I wanted to believe I still had a chance to court her, so I accepted her turndown with grace.

Because she might have begun to feel stalked if not cornered, and therefore might reject my fourth invitation by setting her hair on fire, I brooded weeks before asking her to accompany me to an event that she was already required to attend. Year after year, she had been president of her school class; therefore, I invited her to the junior-class dance.

When she declined, claiming to be busy on the night, I appealed to her in what I remember as an earnest tone, although as an honest memoirist, I must acknowledge it was more likely a pathetic whine: "But you *have* to go to the dance, it's the *junior-class* dance, and you're the junior-class *president*."

"Oh," she said, "I'm going. But I have to spend the first part of the evening selling tickets at the door. Then I operate the record player for a shift, then I sell refreshments for a shift, and then I clean up the gym."

I declared that those were my top four favorite things to do on a date, which left her no way to be rid of me other than to beat me with her purse or scream for the police.

She smiled and said, "All right." In her soft voice, those words sounded like a declaration of undying love. Because at that moment nothing was hanging from the end of my nose, I felt as suave as Cary Grant.

Eventually I would learn that her father, Bedford's shoemaker, immigrated to the States from Italy and had many Old World attitudes, including the notion that children should work by the time they were teenagers. Gerda actually had part-time jobs at the dry cleaner and the movie theater, and supplemented those incomes with babysitting. From the age of thirteen, she bought her own clothes or, because she was a good seamstress, purchased the materials to make them.

On our first date, between selling tickets and spinning records and selling refreshments and cleaning the gym, we found time for only one dance, but we shared a lot of laughs.

Nevertheless, after escorting her to her door and saying good night, I worried about the impression I had made. I considered racing home to call her and ask for an official date evaluation, but decided I would appear too needy.

The following day, Sunday, was interminable, as if the rotation of the Earth slowed dramatically. Monday morning, at school, I was lying in wait at Gerda's locker when she appeared in the hall outside her homeroom. I half expected a polite hello and a claim of amnesia regarding the events of Saturday evening. Instead, she professed to have laughed so much during our five hours together that her tummy muscles hurt the next morning.

I always assumed girls found dating me to be painful, but this was *good* pain. We continued to date. And laugh together.

I asked her to marry me, and she did.

Shortly after college, and after our wedding, I went to work in a federal anti-poverty initiative for seven months, long enough to discover that such programs enriched those administering them but otherwise created more poverty. And the low pay extended *my* penury for over half a year.

Although Gerda was a bookkeeper with accounting skills and had worked in a bank for a few years, she couldn't find such employment in the tiny Appalachian town, Saxton, where I taught disadvantaged kids. She took a piecework job in a shoe factory, and boarded a company bus at four o'clock each weekday morning for a forty-five-minute trip over the mountains to the manufacturing plant.

We were married with a few hundred dollars, a used car, and our clothes. Of the few houses for rent in Saxton, one had full indoor plumbing. Having moved up from an outhouse lifestyle a decade before, I was loath to return. Rent was sixty-five dollars per month, more than we could afford, but we scrimped on other things to pay it.

The house had neither a refrigerator nor a stove. We bought a used fridge and an electric hot plate. Without an oven, with a hot plate instead of a cooktop, Gerda prepared wonderful meals and could even bake anything we desired, except pies, because the filling would burn at the bottom and remained uncooked at the top.

Financially, that was an iffy year for us, and we worked long hours. But we were happy because we were together.

From Saxton, we moved to the Harrisburg area, and I taught high-school English for eighteen months before Gerda made me an offer that changed our lives. Writing in my spare time, I had sold a few short stories and two paperback novels. "You want to be a full-time writer," she said. "So quit teaching. I'll support us for five years. If you can't make it in five years, you never will make it."

I sometimes claim that I tried to bargain her up to seven years, but she was a tough negotiator.

All these years later, I am humbled by her faith in me and the love that inspired her offer. Considering our situation at the time—shaky finances, limited prospects, more rejections than acceptances from publishers—her trust seems extraordinary. Although I hope that over the years I have become a man who would make such an offer to her if my talent was for math and *hers* was for words, I am humbled because I was not that good a man in those days.

Growing up in poverty, with psychological and physical violence, always embarrassed by my father's escapades, I became by my twenties a man who needed approval almost as a child needs it. I needed too desperately to prove myself, and as a consequence I made numerous bad decisions in business. I was too eager to trust the untrustworthy, to believe patently false promises, to take bad advice if it came from someone who seemed to be knowledgable—and especially if they manipulated me with praise. Always an excellent judge of character, Gerda knew in every instance where I was going wrong, and she tried gently to steer me away from the current cliff, but I took too many years to realize that the only approval that really mattered—in addition to God's—

was hers. Throughout my adult life, Gerda has been a light to lead me.

When some members of both our families and other acquaintances learned that I now wrote fiction full-time while Gerda brought home the bacon as well as the eggs and potatoes that went with it, they took this development as proof that I was a good-for-nothing like my father. They pitied Gerda—and from time to time needled me.

For Gerda and for me, for so many reasons, failure was not a possibility we could accept. At the end of the five years, she quit her job so that we could work together. She managed our finances, did book research, and relieved me of all the demands of life and business that sapped creative energy and that kept my fingers away from the typewriter.

By then, we were making a respectable living but not a fortune. During the *next* five years, the quality of what I wrote improved, but progress in craft and art was seldom matched by increased financial rewards. After a Pennsylvania spring in which we never saw blue sky for forty days—very biblical—we had moved to California for the better weather, and incidentally because of opportunities to do screenwriting. In my early Hollywood ventures, however, I found the film business unfulfilling and depressing. We knew that novelists come and go, that if I did not become essential to a publisher's bottom line, I would sooner rather than later be one of those who had gone and was forgotten.

By 1980, success began to come. Twenty-nine years later, as I write this, worldwide sales of my novels are approaching four hundred million copies. Critics have been largely kind, readers even kinder.

Besides a passion for the English language and an abiding love of storytelling, success required persistence and countless hours of hard work. The central experience of my life and of Gerda's has been hard work, at least sixty hours a week, often seventy, sometimes more.

Our faith tells us that when the last hour comes, the best places to be taken are while in prayer or while engaged in work to which we committed ourselves in cheerful acceptance of the truth that work is the lot of humanity, post Eden. If done with diligence and integrity, work is obedience to divine order, a form of repentance.

For many years, as we gave ourselves to work, we talked about getting a dog. Even in the days when we were on a tight budget, we surrounded ourselves with beauty—cheap posters instead of original oil paintings, carnival glass instead of Daum vases—because beauty soothes the troubled mind and inspires. A dog can be a living work of art, a constant reminder of the exquisite design and breathtaking detail of nature, beauty on four paws. In addition, year by year, we became more aware that this world is a deeply mysterious place, and nothing confirmed the wonder of existence more than what we saw happening between dogs and people with disabilities at Canine Companions for Independence. Being guardians and companions of a dog would be one way to explore more fully the mystery of this world.

We knew that dogs are not well loved if kept largely in the yard, that they are pack animals born to live within a family, and that a dog therefore requires almost as much time as a child. We hesitated to take the plunge because of our work schedules and because after more than three decades of marriage, we had a rhythm to our life that worked and that we feared disrupting.

But in September of 1998, a dog finally entered our lives. Over the subsequent nine years, she often amazed us, frequently astonished us, always delighted us, and in time evoked in us a sense of wonder that will remain with us for the rest of our lives. As any man or woman is not only a man or a woman but is also a spirit corrupted in minor or major ways, so this dog was not only a dog, but also a spirit uncorrupted as no human spirit can be. Of all the agents of this world that have changed me for the better, this dog takes second place only to Gerda, and she brought as much to Gerda as to me.

This dog was as joyful as the most joyful of her kind. She possessed all the many virtues of her species. She was as direct as all dogs are. But she was uncannily intelligent, as well, and in a most undoglike way, she was also at all times mysterious and capable of a solemn behavior that was not merely mood, that was a ceremonial solemnity, as though she observed an important truth implicit in the moment and wished for you to recognize it as well. Gerda and I were not the only ones to witness this behavior, and the more that I grew aware of it and heard it remarked upon by others, the more I became open to the changes this special dog would make in me.

Along came Trixie.

III

anticipation, adventure, and anal glands

SHE ARRIVED WITH her name. Trixie. I joked sometimes that it sounded more like a stripper than a dog. They told us we could change it and that she could quickly be taught to answer to a new name. But if it sounded more like a stripper than a dog, it sounded more like an elf or a fairy than a stripper. Elves and fairies are magical beings; and so was she.

Trixie came to us not as a puppy but as a highly educated and refined young lady of three. As a consequence of elbow surgery, she had taken early retirement from a career as an assistance dog to a beautiful young woman, Jenna, who had lost both legs in a traffic accident. Trixie went into service just as Jenna began the student-teaching portion of her senior year at college, and made quite an impression in an elementary-school classroom.

Since 1990, Gerda and I have been supporters of the Southwest Chapter of Canine Companions for Independence. This remarkable organization raises and trains assistance dogs of four kinds.

A dog in a "service team" is paired with an adult or adolescent with physical disabilities—paraplegics, quadriplegics—and performs tasks such as calling elevators, opening doors, picking up dropped items that a person in a wheelchair can't reach. . . . Some adults who could not live alone before receiving a CCI dog achieve independence; children in wheelchairs gain confidence—and a new best friend.

In a "skilled-companion team," a dog is matched with a child or an adult with a physical or developmental disability, and with that person's primary caretaker, which is usually a parent. The dog helps with various tasks but primarily provides companionship, establishing a deep bond of love. The effect these dogs can have on an autistic child or one with cri du chat is nothing less than miraculous.

A dog in a "hearing team" alerts his deaf or hard of hearing companion to alarm clocks, smoke alarms, doorbells, and other sounds.

"Facility team" dogs are paired with teachers, rehabilitation specialists, or caregivers in hospitals, in classrooms full of kids with developmental disorders, in nursing homes. . . . These dogs work miracles every day.

The assistance dogs given by CCI to people with disabilities do great work because of their training, but their most exceptional achievements may be a consequence of their qualities as *dogs*.

Tom Hollenstein, a friend and board member of CCI's Southwest Chapter, suffered a major spinal injury in a bicycle accident when he was twenty-four. A tall, handsome, personable guy, Tom found himself in a wheelchair, living with his parents again. He is one of the most highly motivated people I've ever met, and he could not long endure a lack of independence. With his first assistance dog, Weaver, Tom took control of his life, moved out of his parents' house into his own apartment, landed a job, and never looked back. Weaver was something special, and one of those human-dog bonds formed that was even deeper than usual. Tom has said that, given the choice of never having been disabled or never having known Weaver, he would choose the dog and therefore the spinal injury. Tom does not speak about such things lightly; he means what he says. He told me that when he lost his four-legged companion, he discovered, in his grief, depths of emotion that he had not realized were in him.

I first read about CCI when I was researching a novel, *Midnight,* that included a character in a wheelchair. I was so taken with the organization's work that I specified the fictional dog, Moose, was CCI-trained. *Midnight,* my first book to reach number one on the best-seller list, caught CCI's attention, and they asked if I would add a paragraph to the end of the paperback edition to promote them and to provide the address of their national headquarters in Santa Rosa, California. I was happy to oblige, and this led to our personal involvement with the Southwest Chapter, long before Trixie was born.

At two and a half, Trixie retired from her assistance work with Jenna, but at three, she became an assistance dog of another kind with Gerda and me. She mended us in many ways.

The director of the Southwest Chapter of CCI, at that time a woman named Judi Pierson, had often encouraged Gerda and me to take a release dog from their program. Not every puppy has the talent, temperament, or physical qualifications to get all the way through the two years of training that leads to graduation.

A puppy raiser, always a volunteer qualified by CCI, raises the dog from its eighth week, after it is turned in by the breeder. The puppy raiser, who has the dog for approximately sixteen months, teaches it to sit, stay, lie down, heel, walk on a loose leash, toilet on command, and other basic tasks.

Thereafter, if the dog has done well, it goes to the CCI campus for six months of more intense training, during which it will acquire more skills than I possess, a statement that anyone who knows me will confirm without hesitation.

If the dog fails out for any reason, it is offered to the person who raised it.

These folks are amazing. To rear and train one of these animals is to fall in love with it—yet these volunteers routinely return their charges to CCI for advanced training and often take another puppy, putting themselves through the loss again because they believe in this organization. Some have raised twenty or more dogs, and it is awe-inspiring to consider how many lives they have changed.

Sometimes the puppy raisers are not able to fit one more pooch in their house, or their circumstances have changed. Then a home must be found for the dog that is being released from the program.

Year after year, as Judi urged us to take a CCI release, we longed to say yes, but we were concerned that we could not give the dog the time and attention it needed. We kept telling Judi—and each other—that we were too busy, that we would have to wait until my writing career entered a quieter phase.

In August of 1998, I completed *Seize the Night,* the sequel to my novel *Fear Nothing,* one of many of my books in which a dog is among the cast of principal characters. Every time I wrote a story that included a canine, my yearning for a dog grew. Readers and critics alike said I had an uncanny knack for writing convincingly about dogs and even for writing from a dog's point of view. When a story contained a canine character, I always felt especially inspired, as if some angel watching over me was trying to tell me that dogs were a fundamental part of my destiny if only I would listen.

At dinner one evening near the end of the month, I raised the subject with Gerda: "We keep saying we're too busy to add a dog to our lives, but I'm afraid we're going to be ninety years old and *still* too busy. Maybe we should just do it, busy or not, and make it work."

We never had children. Since Gerda and I set up shop in 1974, we had been together every day, virtually all day, for twenty-four years. We were apart only twice in thirty-two years of marriage. We were a tight team, and we were daunted by the prospect of having another person in the house. We knew that a dog, no less than a child, would be a person.

At the end of dinner, we were agreed. We weren't ready for a dog, but we were going to *make* ourselves ready.

In September, I called Judi and told her the next time they had a release dog to place, we would give it a home.

She said, "What kind of dog do you want—a mooshy one or a not-mooshy one?"

Because mooshy sounded slightly disgusting, I assumed I wanted a not-mooshy. Apparently, I was not as informed about dog terminology as I thought I was, so I decided to ask for a definition.

"A Labrador retriever wouldn't be a mooshy dog," Judi explained. "The breed has a huge amount of energy and always likes to be *doing* something. A golden retriever, however, is playful and energetic when it wants to be, but is also happy just lying around, observing or cuddling or snoozing. A golden retriever is a mooshy dog."

I had always admired goldens for their beautiful coats, their comic-gentle-noble faces, and their sweet temperaments. I was fifty-three years old, and although I exercised regularly and still had a thirty-inch waist, the indefatigable American Association of Retired Persons already harassed me monthly with their mailers, insisting that I should recognize I was in denial, should face the fact of my mortality, and should join them to receive all the senior-citizen discounts, denture-adhesive analyses, and funeral planning that they stood ready to provide. I decided that a mooshy dog was exactly—and perhaps only—what I could handle.

Judi said that CCI had several goldens being released from the program. Finding a good one would be easy. She was about to leave on a two-week vacation, and we arranged for her to bring the dog to our house on Newport Harbor, rather than to our main residence, in two weeks.

We had bought the beach house to induce ourselves to take most weekends off. We had become workaholics, stuck in the tar pits of our home offices seven days a week. The hassles of packing and traveling even to a place as near as Santa Barbara had come to outweigh the benefits of getting away, and we had ceased to be able to resist the pull of work when we were at home.

The beach was a different environment from where we lived in the hills, yet we could drive there in less than half an hour. If we kept clothes and personal items at the second house and never had to pack to go there, if we took no work with us, we could break free of the grindstone. Between Friday afternoon and Sunday evening, we would relax by the water, and then return rested to the house on the hill.

That was the theory.

Our beach house was on Balboa Peninsula Point, featured a pier and dock on Newport Harbor, was designed by a brilliant architect, Paul Williams, and was constructed in 1936. We remodeled the house, took it back to its Art Deco roots, furnished it, and looked forward to mere fifty-hour workweeks.

To a person, friends and relatives who stayed there called the beach house magical and said it was the most restful place they had ever been. In the six years that we owned it, Gerda and I managed to stay in our getaway just thirty nights. Vito and Lynn, Gerda's brother and sister-in-law, coming all the way from Michigan, enjoyed the house more nights in those six years than we did.

We have been so long at the grindstone that we've developed an abiding affection for it: the smell of wet granite, the soft rumble as the wheel turns and turns, the tickle as it gently abrades the nose. I am fortunate that I am enchanted by language and find meaning in my work.

As the day of Trixie's arrival approached, the beach house was new enough to us that we still believed we would spend lazy weekends in our pier pavilion, sipping wine, leisurely studying AARP brochures regarding the benefits of fiber and the dangers of driving faster than twenty miles an hour.

Even by that time, I had written several books in which canines were featured in major or supporting roles—from *Watchers* to *Dragon Tears,* and our friends knew how much we wanted a dog. They also knew that Gerda and I were long accustomed to being a family of two, and some expected that we would have difficulty sharing each other as completely as a dog would require.

The morning of the day when Trixie would arrive, I visited the construction site where we were building a new house. Our general contractor, Mike Martin, was a friend who became like a brother to Gerda and me during the course of this long project. Mike stood six feet four and seemed even taller by virtue of his personality; big and strong, gentle and soft-spoken, quick to laugh, white-haired at fifty, he dressed always in white sneakers, blue jeans, and one Reyn Spooner Hawaiian shirt or another. Mike was charismatic but self-effacing, a combination I have encountered only a few times in my life, and he cared deeply about his friends. As we stepped out of the construction trailer to have a look at whatever problem had brought me to the site, Mike said with concern, "You know, with a dog, any dog, even one of these CCI dogs, things aren't going to be as neat as you like them. It's going to make you a little crazy."

Gerda and I have a reputation among friends for being unusually neat and orderly. I've never quite understood this, because none of our friends is slovenly and disordered by comparison with us. Mike and his wife, Edie, had two dogs yet kept an immaculate home. As a creator of exquisite hot rods, he was obsessive about detail, which is evident in every square foot of the house he built for us. Yet here he was, with his usual concern, warning me that any dog we took in would inevitably bring with it enough disorder to put me at risk of a mental breakdown.

It is true that we fold our socks rather than roll them, that we iron our underwear, that for years I would not wear jeans that didn't have a crease pressed into them, that prior to a dinner party I use a tape measure to ensure precisely the same distance between each place setting (and between each element of each place setting), that Gerda would rather be coated in honey and staked out on an anthill than go to bed when there's even one dirty spoon in the kitchen sink, and that if a guest discovered water spots on a wineglass, we would be no less mortified than if he had found someone's body compressed into a cube in our trash compactor. None of this means that we're obsessive. It means only that we *care*.

In response to Mike's concern that we were too oriented toward order and neatness to cope with a golden retriever, I said, "This dog is well trained, totally housebroken."

"I'm not talking about that kind of thing," Mike said.

"We know it sheds. We'll give it a long combing every morning."

"I'm not thinking about dog hair."

"It'll go to a groomer for a bath and the full works every

Thursday, so I'll never have to express its anal glands myself."

"I'm not thinking about that stuff, either," Mike said, "though I usually do think of anal glands when I think of you."

"You're fired," I said.

"I'd be worried," he said, "except who else would want to work for you?"

"Maybe someone who's actually built a house before," I replied.

Prior to committing himself to the ten years of planning and construction that our house required—including four years with three architects before the third one delivered what we wanted—Mike had been a mason and then a swimming-pool contractor. Our house was the first he built, and the two architects whose plans we did not use were always trying to get him fired, which is one of the reasons that Gerda and I let *them* go.

Over the years, we have learned that the most important quality anyone can possess is character. If a person has true character—which always includes a sense of honor and duty, as well as a tough set of personal standards—he or she will not fail you. Experience matters, but an experienced homebuilder without character is forever a trapdoor under your feet, waiting to be sprung. When we asked Mike if he could take on a project as complex as this one, he said yes without hesitation, and we hired him with confidence. We never had a regret.

Now on the morning of Trixie's arrival, in the affectionate mockery that is a characteristic of our relationships with most of Gerda's and my friends, Mike said, "By neat, I mean your days won't be as structured as you're used to, and your time won't be used as efficiently anymore. You'll find out what it's like being a normal person after all these years of being so damned *abnormal*."

I said, "I think of myself as *delightfully* abnormal."

"Yeah, right," Mike said.

"The dog," I predicted, "will not bring a tenth as much chaos into my life as you have, and because she'll be bathed once a week, she'll also smell better."

"It's happening again," he said. "I'm thinking of anal glands."

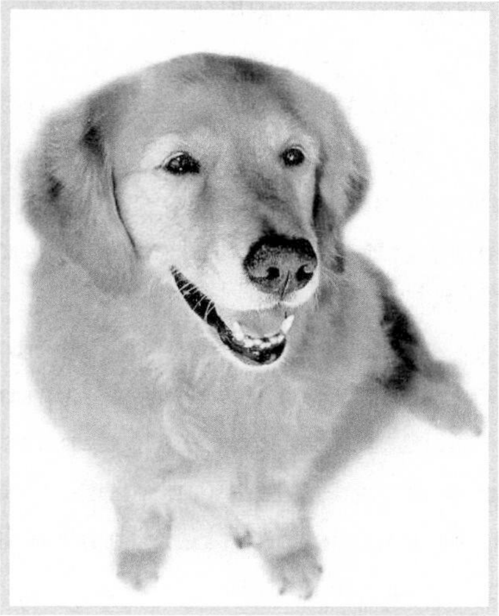

IV

"if this dog does something wrong, the fault will be yours, not hers"

LINDA, A COMPUTER maven and all-around talent, has been Gerda's and my primary assistant for so long that she will need to be in therapy for the rest of her life.

On the other hand, before she came to us, she did contract work for the state of California, instructing bureaucrats in the software they used. California government is so dysfunctional, by comparison with Koontzland, that it must have seemed like an asylum to Linda, while our little corner of the world might well have struck her as a restful sanitarium.

Back in 1998, Linda occupied an office in our house on the hill. But our second assistant, Elaine, who had come to us after retiring from another job, worked in our office suite in a commercial complex called Newport Center.

Linda and Elaine had asked if they could meet Trixie when we did. They were friends as well as employees, and the addition of a dog to our lives made them happy for us. Besides, they were always looking for one reason or another to skip work, and this was a much better excuse than claiming for the sixteenth time that a beloved grandmother or beloved aunt had died.

Also with us were Vito and his wife, Lynn, visiting from Michigan and staying in the beach house for two weeks. They had a dog they loved, a not-mooshy Labrador retriever named Rocky, so we figured they could help us adjust to our new daughter.

Judi arrived with Trixie's puppy raiser, Julia Shular, who also had with her a black Labrador in training for CCI. They had all of Trixie's favorite toys, a bag of her kibble, and what seemed like 9,324 pages of instructions on her care.

Joint surgery will force the retirement of any assistance dog because, in a pinch, it might need to pull its partner's wheelchair. Even after healing, the problem joint puts the animal at risk. Having recuperated for six months, our daughter was fully recovered.

When Trixie entered the house off leash, she had a sprightly step and an eager, inquisitive expression. Tail swishing, she came directly to Gerda and me, as if she had been shown photographs of us and knew we were to be her new mom and dad. Then she politely visited with Linda, Elaine, Vito, and Lynn, sharing the fur.

Cynics will tell you that love at first sight is a myth, but their opinion is not to be respected, and only reveals the sad condition of their hearts.

We fell in love with Trixie at first sight, in part because of her beauty. Her mother, Kinsey, was a gorgeous specimen, and her father, Bugs—Kinsale Bugaboo Boy—was a winner of multiple dog-show prizes. Her grandfather Expo also had been a show-dog champion. Trixie had a good broad face, correct ear size and placement, dark eyes, and a black nose without mottling. Her head and neck flowed perfectly into a strong level topline, and her carriage was regal.

Beauty took second place, however, to her personality. Although well behaved, with a gentle and affectionate temperament, she had about her a certain cockiness, as well. During that first meeting, she seemed always to be either laughing or ready to laugh, and Judi said she had been the class clown of her graduating group.

Because the male Labrador remained in training, Trixie took advantage of her new status as an ordinary dog to tease him and to tempt him to break his sit-stay. While we listened to Judi and Julia instruct us in Trixie's basic commands, we watched our girl take three different toys to the Lab and hold them inches from his face, jubilantly squeaking them to impress on him what fun he was missing.

Her favorite toy was what we called a dangle ball, a big fuzzy ball dangling on a loop of braided rope. She swung this in front of the Lab's face, like a hypnotist swinging a pendant on a chain, and when he let his mouth sag open, tempted to make a grab for the toy, Trixie stepped back, insisting that he break his sit-stay.

In spite of our girl's clownish tendency, we supposedly would rarely need to correct her behavior. Judi said that Trixie was so well trained and so smart that "if this dog does something wrong, the fault will be yours, not hers, because you will have gotten a command wrong or will have forgotten to do some part of her daily routine that she requires to stay on her schedule."

Linda and Elaine left, not to return to work, as we might have hoped, but to make funeral arrangements for beloved aunts who had died that morning. What a sad world this is, with so much death.

When Judi and Julia left a few minutes later, Trixie set off to explore every corner of the house, bottom to top and down again. She would repeat this practice over the years in every friend's house to which she was invited. With one exception, she never took liberties with anything in those homes, but her curiosity was matched only by her assumption that she was welcome to snoop everywhere.

Vito, Lynn, Gerda, and I took Trixie with us to dinner that evening at a restaurant that welcomed dogs on its patio. When given the command "under," she settled under the table, facing out, and watched the other diners. She showed no interest in our food, was never restless, and made no sound.

Later in the evening, we brought her for the first time to our house on the hill, and she at once explored it as she had explored the beach house. We put her bed in a corner of the master bedroom, and she settled into it. Although we invited her to sleep at the bottom of our bed, and although she'd had some furniture privileges in her previous homes, she preferred the familiarity of her dog bed.

As we were lying in the dark, waiting for sleep, Gerda said, "A little scary, huh?"

I knew what she meant: The responsibility for this beautiful creature was now ours alone. Her health, her happiness, and the maintenance of the training that made her not only an ideal canine but also contributed to her confidence and to her sense of her place in the world—those things we must attend to no less dutifully than we would have tended to the needs of a child.

Sometime during the night, I woke with the feeling that I was being watched. Gerda and I sleep in a pitch-black room, where the windows are covered by wooden panels at night. I didn't want to switch on the flashlight that I keep on my nightstand, so still lying on my side, I squinted in search of animal eyeshine, but could see none. Tentatively, I reached out past the side of the bed with my right hand, and at once found Trixie's head. For a couple of minutes, in the dark, I rubbed the sensitive part of one of her ears between my thumb and index finger, and she leaned into this caress. Then she sighed and returned to her bed in the corner, and soon slept.

I imagined she had stood there, breathing in my complex scent, analyzing me with her talented nose, asking herself if I would be kind to her and love her and be worth loving in return. I intended never to give her reason to answer no to any of those questions.

V

if she could talk, she'd do stand-up comedy

NOT LONG AFTER Trixie came to live with us, Judi sent a photograph of our girl with the rest of the dogs in her CCI class. "I don't need to identify Trixie for you," she said. "You'll have no trouble recognizing her."

In the photo, a dozen dogs face the camera in a semicircle. Most are goldens and hard to tell apart in a photograph, but a few are Labradors. Eleven of the dogs sit erect, in stately poses, chests out, heads raised, each holding the end of its leash in its mouth as proof of its high degree of learning.

The twelfth dog sits with legs akimbo, grinning, head cocked, a comic portrait of a clownish canine, ready for fun. This obvious free spirit is Trixie.

A trainer told us that when Trixie and her classmates were being taught the stay command, Trixie learned it quicker than the rest. At that point, further lessons on the same subject became a chance for her to have fun.

After the dogs seemed to learn to stay, all the trainers went into the adjacent room, closing the door behind them, leaving not one human in sight. Between rooms, a view window on the trainers' side was a mirror from the dogs' perspective. The teachers could watch the students and learn how long each maintained the stay.

For a minute, all the dogs did well. Then Trixie surveyed the room to make doubly sure no human had returned, and she broke her stay. She went to each of her classmates, one by one, and tried to tease him or her into joining the rebellion.

One of the trainers rattled the doorknob. Trixie sprang back to her original position, as if she had never disobeyed the command.

Until all the dogs in the class had learned to hold the stay, Trixie played the temptress. Frequently she induced a few classmates to break their positions, but at the rattle of the doorknob, she sprinted to her place and sat with her chest out and head raised, letting her pals take the fall.

Many incidents confirmed that Trixie had a sense of humor and suggested an uncanny level of intelligence, but my favorite occurred one night when we went to our friend—and assistant—Elaine's house for dinner. By this time, we had moved into our new home and closed our offices in Newport Center. Elaine now worked in our house with Linda, and Trixie spent hours every day in their office.

I'm reluctant to compliment Elaine in this account because she'll take it as a sign of weakness. Around here, giving anyone too many compliments brings out in that person the same predatory instinct that energizes a hungry lion when it glimpses a limping gazelle. My kind words will earn me much mockery not only from all our friends who know Elaine but also from Elaine herself. I must admit, however, that being a target can be as much fun as dishing it out.

Anyway, here goes: She is an attractive lady with lovely blue eyes, much older than anyone would believe, very much older, beyond my powers of calculation, but it is her personality that wins her so many friends and makes them so loyal to her. Elaine genuinely likes people, and she is sincerely interested in the lives of everyone she meets.

When Elaine worked for us, she went to the post office every day, to Federal Express and the office-supply store, and numerous other places, in part because we wanted her out of the house as much as possible, but also in part because we never had to worry that Elaine would be unkind to anyone or impatient with anyone. When you are even to a small degree a public figure, it is especially important that the people interacting with the world on your behalf should be liked and respected by everyone with whom they deal. Long after Elaine retired from her position with us and even after we finally were able to expunge the peculiar stains from the limestone floor around her desk, people everywhere that she went on our behalf were still asking about her, still under the spell of her inexplicable charm.

One thing that particularly fascinates Elaine's friends is that every man she has ever dated, considered dating, or rejected without dating remains in touch with her and continues to adore her. Even those beaus who served in the Spanish-American War and can no longer recall their own names nonetheless vividly remember Elaine. She has turned down marriage proposals, and those whose hearts she's broken with a smile continue to be her hopeful admirers, their infatuation undiminished by her rejection.

A gentleman named Al almost convinced Elaine to join him at the altar. In the end, however, he met the same fate that is visited upon all her suitors and was let down gently; this is better than having your head bitten off, which is what the female praying mantis does to its male companions, but it still hurts. Even after he had been torpedoed by Elaine, Al continued sending her flowers, candy, and other gifts to express his abiding love. One of the things he gave her was a cowboy doll that, when squeezed, played Billy Ray Cyrus singing "Achy Breaky Heart." Elaine thought this gift was sweet, though her friends—

well, the few with taste—thought that perhaps she had done a wise thing when she had moved on from Al to destroy the last desperate romantic dreams of myriad other men of advanced age.

Elaine threw a dinner party for a group of us who were all friends and former neighbors of one another. As always, she invited Trixie, whom she saw every day at work and sometimes walked. Everyone who met Trixie loved her, just as everyone loved Elaine, a fact that I have often brooded about without deciding on its meaning.

Dinner that evening was not served until ten thirty because Elaine had forgotten to turn on the oven after putting the roast in it. She looked through the view window a few times, upset that the meat would not cook, before she noticed the oven was off. None of us in attendance—and starving—found this development surprising. Elaine can spend ten minutes looking for the car keys that she's holding in her hand. Lest you worry that her occasional confusion indicates the onset of Alzheimer's, people who knew her when she was a teenager tell us that even then she could spend ten minutes searching for the horses to pull the covered wagon when the poor beasts were already standing in their traces and ready to go.

When you start drinking red wine at six o'clock, expecting dinner at seven thirty, and when dinner arrives three hours later than promised, you are in a very forgiving mood and find the chef to be as adorable as do the uncountable men whom she has discarded like old shoes. Conversation around the dinner table was lively if not raucous, and surprisingly coherent, considering. About halfway through the meal, someone asked Elaine if she had heard from Al lately, and before she could reply, from under the table came the voice of Billy Ray Cyrus singing "Achy Breaky Heart," as if Al were under there, concealed by the tablecloth.

Trixie, when visiting a friend, never before or thereafter appropriated the property of the host for her own use, but with her timely addition of a soundtrack, she got the biggest laugh of the night, and came out from under the table to accept applause.

Any Spot or Fido might decide that a colorfully outfitted cowboy doll must be a dog toy. Settling with it under the dinner table would also be predictable dog conduct.

But Trixie had stood on her hind feet to pluck the doll off a shelf that she could barely reach. Instead of munching it at once and activating the recording, she took it quietly under the table, without anyone seeing her. That she bit the song from it *precisely* when someone asked Elaine if she'd heard from Al lately . . .

Well, I won't go so far as to say that this uncanny canine knew Al had given the doll to Elaine, that she bided her time and waited to hear Al's name, that she knew why this would strike all present as hilarious. For suggesting such a thing, I would no doubt attract the attention of the Bureau for the Compassionate Care of the Inadvisably Mystic-Minded or some other government agency that would want to lock me up for my own good. But as with so many things about Trixie, this moment at a dinner party was magical and uncanny.

Trixie was a joker, all right, and when she wasn't lying in wait under a table for a laugh, other furniture inspired her humor. A console, a dresser, a sideboard, any item on short legs intrigued her. She would stand with head lowered, sniffing the narrow space under the piece. By her urgent attitude, she seemed to say that she had trapped a critter and that we ought to have a look at what she cornered. If we didn't take her suggestion right away, she would lie down and paw at whatever might be in the hidden space.

Inevitably, when we got warily on our hands and knees to peer under the furniture for the mouse, nothing was there. The way Short Stuff grinned at us, I swear this was her idea of a practical joke. We fell for it again and again, and when we refused to be conned, we saw her pull the trick on other people.

In the Harbor Ridge house, we once had a real mouse loose on the lowest of three floors. In the kitchen, I lined up a series of mousetraps in the lid of a box that I could carry to the lower floor, and I baited them with chunks of cheese, one by one.

Trixie stood at the counter, at my side, interested in my task but drawn also by the aroma of Velveeta. Five times, as I carefully put down a set trap, it sprang, flipping into the air with a hard snap, which caused Trixie to twitch but didn't frighten her into flight. The sprung traps cast bits of cheese to the floor, which Trix snatched up with pleasure.

In truth, I shouldn't be allowed any nearer to a mousetrap than to an armed nuclear device. I'm no more mechanically inclined than I am gifted at bird imitations.

After I carried the traps downstairs and placed them, I decided I needed four or five more. My strategy when I am out to kill a mouse is not to trust in its taste for cheese. Should it be that rare mouse disgusted by the very idea of cheese, I distribute so many traps in each small area that the little beast will inevitably blunder into a deadly mechanism the first time it ventures from cover.

In the kitchen again, where Trixie waited, I put five more traps in the box lid. She watched me solemnly, but instead of waiting for more cheese to be flung by sprung traps, she made a low throaty noise of concern and backed away from me, tail between her legs. She backed across the kitchen and through the doorway to the family room, and kept backing away, away, in my line of sight, until she was at the farther end of that adjacent room, fully forty feet from where she had started. Once there, she made several wheezing sounds that were as close to laughter as I can imagine a dog getting. Her tail began to wag, and she grinned at me.

I know as surely as I know anything that she was having fun at my expense, mocking my mechanical ineptitude with the easily sprung traps. She was saying, *I really want the dropped cheese, Dad, but I want to live, too, so I'm getting out of the death zone.*

•

G. K. Chesterton—who had two dogs, Winkle and Quoodle—wrote more than a little about the importance of laughter in a well-lived life, and of laughter's role in a marriage, he said: "A man and a woman cannot live together without having against each other a kind of everlasting joke. Each has discovered that the other is not only a fool, but a great fool." Dogs love to play the fool, and as part of the family, they are quite capable of recognizing the fool in us, and of celebrating it with a joke now and then.

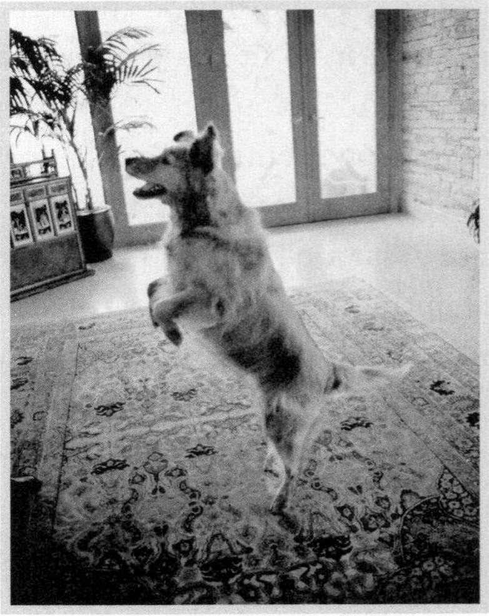

VI

she poops on command, but not just anywhere

DURING THOSE FIRST days with Trixie, we learned that her personal tao, the code of virtuous conduct by which she lived, included a proscription against pooping on our property. She would pee on our lawn, but she refused to do the nastier act within the borders of our domain. She lived with us for eight years, nine months, and five days, and not once in all that time did she break this self-imposed rule, which had nothing to do with her training.

As part of CCI's excellent instruction, their canine graduates obey a toileting command. When you speak this word, they do number one and then number two (if they need to), with nearly as much dispatch as they sit or lie down when given one of those commands.

Considering the many tasks these dogs can perform, I was for a while surprised that people unfamiliar with CCI were routinely most amazed by the toileting command. "It's astonishing," friends would say, and then at once wonder, "but why would anyone even think to teach a dog such a thing?"

The answer is that a person in a wheelchair is not easily able to escort a canine companion outside at the animal's whim. It's more convenient for them if the dog is fed on a strictly observed schedule that establishes a daily toileting rhythm. If in addition they can speak a command that encourages the dog to do its business promptly, instead of waiting while it wanders around in search of precisely the best spot to leave its treasure, all the better.

Trixie needed to toilet after breakfast in the morning, again between eleven o'clock and noon, again after her three thirty meal, and just before bed. Overnight, she could wait twelve hours, if necessary, without a need to visit Mother Nature.

Because she had an hour-long walk each morning and a half-hour walk in the afternoon, we didn't always employ the toileting command, and she did not absolutely *require* that we give it. She realized we were allowing her some license in the matter on the longer walks.

But even if we gave the command while on our property, she would refuse to do more than pee. After she had done number one, if we then repeated the command, encouraging her to proceed to number two, she would stare at us in disbelief, as if to say, *What—are you kidding me? This is our home, we* live *here.*

We are blue-baggers. We always pick up after our dog and double-bag it, whether we're on our property, a neighbor's, or in a park. Regardless of where Trixie did number two, we collected it, so she *knew* we weren't going to leave it where it dropped. When returning from a walk, we always went directly to our trash enclosure to put the filled bags in the proper can. Gerda would often say to Trixie, "We have to stop at Bank of America and make your deposit," and it seemed to me that our furry daughter knew this was a joke, as she would wag her tail and grin.

Our house on the hill had an ocean view, and like many such communities in southern California, the lots were on the small side because the land value was prohibitive. On the view side of the residence, we had no lawn, only patios, but on the street side, a modest breadth of grass offered any dog an appealing lavatory. Any dog but Trixie, who insisted always that she must cross our property line before proceeding to the more momentous half of her potty routine.

The beach house required of her a more complicated analysis in order to live by her toilet tao. The back of the house, which faced the water, had no lawn, only patios and a sandy beach. The front of the house faced on a street so narrow that it was more properly called an alley, though I heard it referred to as a lane, a court, and a gallery by those who didn't want people to think that their front door must be flanked by Dumpsters against which winos slept. Across this alley, behind our house, lay three lots that were also part of the property. Here were grass, gardens, and lemon trees. Often, I commanded Trixie to relieve herself in this green haven, but intuitively she knew this was still part of our grounds, and she would not squat.

A high wall separated those gardens from the public street to which, inevitably, I would have to lead her. Between the street and the public sidewalk, a four-foot-wide greensward offered grass and trees. The city required us to mow and keep healthy the grass in this public greensward, for the length that it paralleled our lots. Other neighbors had to tend their portions of the strip, and some of them replaced the grass with bricks, for easier maintenance.

Although this narrow green belt was not our property, Trixie seemed to know it nonetheless remained our responsibility. That was enough to make it a no-poop zone. We had to walk her to a neighbor's portion of the strip or across the street to a pocket park, before she would proceed with the second half of her potty.

How this dog could know where our land ended and where that of a neighbor began, I do not know. But she had such a precise sense of property lines that she needed to take just one step across the boundary before she would heed nature's call.

The funniest toilet-tao incident was also deeply touching. It occurred during a four-week period when she vomited routinely at least once or twice a day. Previously, she had not been a sickly dog in that sense, and her condition greatly worried us.

By this time, we had sold the house on the hill and had moved into our current home, which is the first house we ever built from the ground up. We are on two and a half acres, so Trixie had abundant room to run and play.

When she began to suffer stomach problems, the awful sound of her retching woke us in the middle of the night. A few times, she threw up on the light-beige carpet in the master suite, and this clearly distressed her. Outside of the master suite, most floors in this house are honed limestone with a matte sealer. If she could wake us in time, she waited for us to open the bedroom door, raced down the stairs, and disgorged on limestone, where the mess could be cleaned up more easily and without leaving a stain.

As the reader must now realize, this is not going to be a memoir about a pillow-destroying, cat-chasing, furniture-chewing, miscreant kind of canine. I did not exaggerate earlier when I said that she was something more than a dog, just as each of us is something more than the physical body we inhabit. This dog, this individual, this furry person, this *spirit* was a wonder and a revelation.

Her veterinarians had difficulty diagnosing the cause of her stomach upset. Even after they decided that we must be dealing with a food allergy, we had to discover by trial and error which food irritated her. By the time we knew it had to be either wheat or beef—and decided to eliminate both from her diet rather than risk one more spell of sickness—we had cleaned up enough vomit to get a spot in the *Guinness Book of World Records,* supposing they would agree to include an upchuck category.

During this period, Trixie's worst episode of each day occurred between two and three o'clock in the morning. As her distress grew, she woke us by coming to our bed in the dark and panting loudly, for she rarely barked and never whimpered.

In the pioneer spirit that impelled each of our forefathers to sleep with a Remington rifle beside the bed and a bowie knife between his clenched teeth, I kept nearby a pair of jeans, shoes, a roll of paper towels, a spray bottle of Nature's Miracle, and a plastic bag. Eventually, counting from the moment Trixie's urgent panting woke me, I could be in my jeans and shoes, with my clean-up gear in hand, ready to follow her to the nearest limestone floor, in 2.23 seconds.

If we'd had some foresight, we could have installed a fireman's pole between the bedroom and the lower floors, enabling me to be waiting for Trixie in the limestone hallway when she reached it by the stairs.

The night that her toilet tao was put to the ultimate test, the clock showed 3:30 a.m. when she woke us. At 3:30:02:21, I was jeaned, shoed, equipped, ready to follow her—a personal best for me.

On this occasion, she raced all the way from the third floor to the first, to the hallway that leads to the garage, where she delivered a reedited version of her dinner kibble. I cleaned this up, stowed it in an odor-trapping OneZip bag, and took it to the trash can in the garage, leaving Trixie lying on her side in what appeared to be a state of exhaustion.

Because sometimes the initial regurgitation was followed by a second and more minor event of the same kind, I took a quilted moving blanket from a garage cabinet and used it as a bed on the hallway floor to make our wait comfortable. Lying face-to-face with Trixie, I stroked her side and spoke softly to reassure her.

That night on the hallway floor, as Trixie and I waited to see if she needed to purge her stomach a second time, that yearning look in her eyes, that seeming desire to speak, was stronger than I had ever seen it before. Suddenly she leaped to her feet, turned from me, and ran into the garage, where I had left the door open.

She had been lethargic for some time because of her sickness, so her energetic exit surprised and then alarmed me. I followed her into the garage, where I saw that she had sprinted to the rack on which we hung her collars and leashes.

She looked from the leashes to me, to the leashes, to me. I realized this food allergy, which previously had been expressed solely through vomiting, was about to have an effect at the other end of the dog. Trixie needed to poop. *Now.*

Quickly, I put on her collar, put my hand through the leash loop, and she took off. As I gasped to keep pace with Trixie, she ran the length of the long garage, to the man door beside the big roll-up.

Just beyond this door was the driveway and, to the left, a large yard graced by a double colonnade of California pepper trees, where we often played fetch with a tennis ball. Although it was nearly four o'clock in the morning, although no one but I would be aware that she violated her toilet tao, Trixie would not trot twenty feet to the pepper-tree lawn and void there. It was, after all, *our* property, sacred territory. Instead, she raced up the driveway, into the night, pulling me with her.

Halfway between the garage and the driveway gate, she turned right, up another length of driveway that led to the motor court. Her toenails click-click-clicked on the quartzite paving, and my feet raised loud slapping sounds as I staggered wildly after her, hoping not to be pulled off balance. She ran across the motor court, down a set of stairs to the front entrance, through the front gate, and up a 160-foot-long wheelchair ramp paralleling the entry stairs that descended to our front door.

This circuitous route equaled at least one and a half football fields. At the end of the breathless journey, Trixie stepped off our property, squatted on our neighbors' front lawn, and instantly had explosive diarrhea.

Standing in the cool night, under a fat moon, I said to her, "You are the best dog in the world. But I *like* our neighbors, so I still have to clean up the mess."

For the remaining years of her life, wheat and beef were removed from Trixie's diet. She never had another bout of gastrointestinal distress. But I was motivated to stay fit just in case she ever again had to make a five-hundred-yard diarrhea run.

On the day we had adopted Trixie, Mike Martin had worried that because of our compulsive neatness and our need for order, we would find our lives disrupted by a dog. Instead, Trix was so fastidious, with such a natural sense of propriety, that we had to rise to her standards.

In the new house, Linda and Elaine shared a large office with plenty of roaming room for Trixie, who spent part of each weekday there because Linda walked her at 11:30 and 3:30.

In addition to the toilet tao that prohibited her from pooping on our property, Trixie was discreet about other matters biological. She did not want us to look at her when she was doing either number one or number two, so we had to stare off into the distance or into the sky, as though contemplating weighty philosophical issues.

She allowed us to bag her leavings, but while we gathered them, she often turned her back or stared off into the distance as though contemplating weighty philosophical issues. The times I caught her watching me at this task, she always appeared incredulous, as if my motives were beyond comprehension.

One afternoon, as Trixie dozed on her dog bed, Linda and Elaine were busy at their desks. Suddenly a ripe aroma filled the room. Neither of them remarked on the smell as it dissipated. But when it bloomed again, Elaine declared, "Linda, dear, please remember, I'm a delicate flower with refined sensibilities. I'm withering here. Whatever you had for dinner last night, never eat it again if the next day is a workday."

"Nice try," Linda said, "but we know which one of us *lives* on Metamucil." When Elaine insisted she was innocent, Linda said, "Well, it isn't me and it certainly isn't Trixie."

At that time, Trix had been with us over seven years, and if she had ever passed gas around any of us, it had been odorless.

Recognizing each other's sincerity, Linda and Elaine exchanged a glance of disbelief, for a moment speechless, then turned their attention to the dog and simultaneously said, *"Trixie?"*

They couldn't have been more shocked if they had seen the Queen of England spit tobacco juice on an antique carpet.

VII

cnn, cci, tv, and tk

AS FAR AS I know, I'm the only writer who has appeared often on the best-seller list but who has never done a national or even a multi-state book-publicity tour. I also have never stabbed my wife, as Norman Mailer stabbed one of his, nor have I dissed Oprah Winfrey, as Jonathan Franzen did, nor have I faked a bad-boy history and invented a colorful past as James Frey did: I am a publicist's worst nightmare.

I dislike most publicity, aside from radio interviews, which I enjoy because of the energy and intelligence of the folks who work in that medium. Besides, I can do six hours of early-morning radio programs with bed hair, without shaving, with sticky-bun stains on my T-shirt, and listeners will assume that I'm as scrubbed and as perfectly coiffed as Donny Osmond on his way to church.

Cubby Greenwich, the writer who is the protagonist of my novel *Relentless,* has my aversion to publicity and explains it better than I can: "Protracted self-promotion drains something essential from the soul, and after one of these sessions, you need weeks to recover and to decide that one day it might be all right to like yourself again."

I do as much publicity as feels fair to my publishers—and as little as I can persuade them is fair. In 1998, I was new to Bantam Books, having published one novel with them and having delivered a second that awaited publication. When they asked me to do the CNN biography program *Pinnacle* to support the release of *Seize the Night,* I probably grumped a little, just so everyone would know what a humongous and debilitating imposition it was, no less traumatic than open-heart surgery, but I agreed.

Trixie had been part of our lives less than a week when the producer, film crew, and program host for *Pinnacle* came to Newport Beach to spend two days with us. Already, we could not imagine life without her.

The day before the CNN folks showed up, Gerda and I took Trixie to meet her veterinarians. She was scheduled for a full physical and, of course, for a bath and grooming to ensure that she was properly fluffed for a national television appearance.

We did not yet realize that our veterinarians would become such an important part of our lives. Good ones give you the confidence to entrust your furball to them, they gentle you through scary crises, and one day they help you to bear a most devastating loss. We found two fine vets in a practice near us: Bruce Whitaker and Bill Lyle.

For almost nine years, Trixie went to their office for medical attention and also once a week to be bathed and groomed by Heidi, for whom she was always quick to present her belly in greeting. Often when we went to pick up Trixie, she was not in the holding area at the back of the facility, but roamed free with the women who worked up front at the receiving station. A couple of years later, Heidi told us that she didn't cage our girl after a bath because by her presence she calmed other dogs that were nervous about being bathed.

On our first visit, we were amused when the receptionist said, "Dr. Whitaker, Trixie Koontz is here for her appointment." Trixie was now Trixie Koontz, officially a part of the family.

A joyful dog elicits from you a long list of nicknames. For a while I occasionally called her TK, but that was soon supplanted by Furface, Short Stuff, Love Puppy, Trix, Trickster, and others.

For the CNN interview, TK was super-fluffed, and throughout the experience, she remained properly unimpressed that she had become part of a celebrity family.

Weeks prior to the *Pinnacle* interview, the producer spoke with me by telephone, walking me through the subjects they might want to discuss. Everything went smoothly until he said, "And because yours is basically a sedentary profession, we'd like to get some footage of you and Gerda engaged in colorful leisure activities."

I explained that aside from having taken six years of ballroom-dancing lessons, we had not done anything colorful. In fact, we strove to avoid the colorful in favor of the comfortable and the safe. We did not sky-dive, wrestle bears, charm snakes, or ride a motorcycle in tandem while wearing horned Viking helmets.

Television thrives on color and movement, so we were at a crisis point. After much mulling, I suggested that *Pinnacle* accompany Gerda and me to Canine Companions for Independence, at its Oceanside campus, because the organization was such an important part of our lives and would offer the producer all the color he needed. Besides, I am always trying to get CCI publicity that will bring them more donations. The producer was baffled and could not imagine what would be visually interesting about assistance dogs and a bunch of people in wheelchairs. He agreed to go with us to Oceanside on the second morning but "just for an hour."

Thereafter, he wanted to return to Newport, where Gerda and I would walk on the beach for the camera and do other semicolorful things. Maybe I could climb a date palm, chase the rats out of their nest at the top of the tree, and even catch one in my teeth. I did not actually suggest the palm-rat-teeth scenario, but I'm sure that if I had, the producer would have sighed with relief and said, *"Yes!"*

To that point, my experiences with the press had been mostly dismaying. In an interview in a major newspaper, a reporter had invented every quote that he put in my mouth, had written that I worked in a windowless room, when in fact it featured an eight-by-five-foot window, and made forty-six other errors of fact in an attempt to make me appear to be an even bigger fool than I am, which itself is a fool's errand. No one can make me appear more foolish than I already am. An artist might as well try to paint a hippopotamus that is *more* of a hippopotamus than the real animal. Given open-minded attention by a reporter, I will be as preposterous as anyone since time immemorial, thereby saving him the need to invent idiocies to attribute to me.

The *Pinnacle* team showed up on schedule, and they were a pleasant surprise. The producer and crew were friendly, considerate, professional, and they all had a sense of humor that put us at ease. Beverly Schuch, the on-camera host and interviewer, was a gracious woman who joined in the crew's joking.

I am publicity-shy, but Gerda is an extremely private person who might want to shoot out the limelights if you directed them at her. I was surprised that the *Pinnacle* folks induced her to participate so fully in the program.

Years after, I enjoyed reviewing the parts of the tape in which she appeared, so lovely on a warm September day.

Trixie, however, had none of Gerda's hesitancy. We learned with *Pinnacle* that she enjoyed the limelight. She did everything asked of her—walk here, walk there, turn this way, sit, smile—as if instead of going through assistance-dog training, she had attended modeling school. She was in fact a camera hound.

Early on the second day with *Pinnacle,* we traveled to the Oceanside campus of Canine Companions for Independence. Gerda's brother, Vito, and his wife, Lynn, were in their second week at the beach house, and they agreed to accompany us to take care of Trixie if we were with the film crew just when Short Stuff's schedule called for food or a bathroom break.

Judi, the Oceanside campus director, gave *Pinnacle* a tour of the facility and encouraged them to film a session with the trainers and the current class of dogs heading toward graduation. Everyone from CNN became so enthralled with CCI that they remained not "just for an hour," as the producer initially envisioned, but for the entire morning and the early afternoon. Later that year, they filmed a one-hour special about CCI that ran in the Christmas season.

During our tour, we came to the kennels, in which puppies were currently housed, all of them eight to ten weeks old and soon to be handed over to the volunteers who would raise them. Judi suggested that Gerda and I go into the play yard between kennels, get on our knees, and meet the puppies, which she would release from their pens with the flip of a switch. In these two days, Gerda had been in front of a camera more than she hoped to be in a lifetime, so she backed off, leaving me to face the ferocious pack alone. When the puppies were released, most proved to be golden retrievers, the others Labradors. They raced exuberantly to me. In an instant, I was wearing a live-puppy coat.

In the care of Vito and Lynn, Trixie watched me go into the fenced kennel and pressed to the chain-link with interest, as if saying, *I used to live here, Dad. But why would you want to? The house on the hill is way better than this.*

Then the puppies exploded into the play yard and clambered over me. I laughed with delight—and Trixie at once turned her back on this display and refused to watch. Vito and Lynn tried to get her to turn to the fence once more, but she clearly disapproved of me cavorting with cute puppies.

We took this to mean that after just a few days, she had bonded with us, and she did not want to consider that she might have to share our affections with another dog. Hour by hour, we were more certainly a family of three.

Long before that day, Oceanside had thoughtfully set aside a large tract from which the city council intended to carve gifts of land to be granted to worthy nonprofit organizations. CCI's Southwest Chapter had previously been quartered in the San Diego area, but had moved north to accept Oceanside's generosity. In a moment between sessions with *Pinnacle,* Gerda and I asked Judi Pierson what CCI intended to do with the substantial portion of their land they had not already built on, and she described a project that intrigued us and that eventually became an important part of our future—and Trixie's.

After returning to Newport Beach that afternoon, we took the *Pinnacle* team to dinner at Zov's Bistro in Tustin, for years our favorite restaurant. Zov didn't have a pro-dog policy, but that day she made an exception and allowed us to bring Trixie. Our golden girl went under the table, facing out, and got up only to lap at a bowl of water.

An hour before the end of dinner, when I glanced down at Trixie to be sure she remained content, I saw her head raised. Something interested her. A piece of chicken the size of a plum lay on the patio floor, twelve inches from her nose. Evidently another diner had tossed it to her, but she was trained to disregard anything that might distract her from the person with disabilities whom she served.

In CCI's large training room, food is sometimes dropped at various places before the day's lesson begins. The dogs then go through their paces, learning to ignore the treats and remain focused on the needs of the trainer who is a sit-in for the wheelchair-bound person with whom the dog will eventually be paired. While in working mode, assistance dogs also must ignore other dogs, as well as cats, rabbits, birds, and anything else they might ordinarily want to chase, such as butterflies and Peterbilts.

On the patio, at dinner with the CNN folks, Trixie was retired, had no person with disabilities to serve, yet she remained faithful to her service-dog tradition. When we left the restaurant an hour later, she had not touched the chicken; as we departed, she stepped over the treat with more pride than regret.

Largely because of the time constraints of a television show, the finished episode of *Pinnacle* got a few things wrong when my answers to some questions were trimmed and spliced. But that had nothing to do with any agenda of theirs and everything to do with my tendency to ramble.

Near the end of the program, pressured by the producer, Gerda and I did a minute or two of swing dancing—without benefit of music, silently counting the beat—to demonstrate the result of all those years of lessons during which I had broken the spirit of more than one dance instructor. This is my favorite moment of the show, not because of our dancing but because the camera slowly zooms in on Trixie, who is watching us intently, as if she has never seen dancing before and as if she is solemnly wondering in what other peculiar rituals her new parents might engage.

VIII

i screw up, dog takes the rap

GOLDEN RETRIEVERS HAVE glorious thick coats, and they shed with exuberance, especially in spring, when they create billowing clouds of fur each time they shake their bodies. Because we preferred not to live in drifts of Trixie's cast-offs, we combed her for half an hour to forty-five minutes after her walk each morning, and another ten or fifteen minutes in the late afternoon or early evening. In addition, every floor in the house was swept at least once a day. No visitor ever saw fur on the floor or went home with more than a few golden filaments on his clothes.

Trixie delighted in these daily grooming sessions, as if they were the doggy equivalent of spa visits. She learned the sequence of the comb-out, and lying on her grooming blanket, she extended a leg just when you needed to comb the feathers on it, rolled from one side to the other with a dreamy sigh. For Gerda and me, grooming this dog qualified as meditation and induced in us a Zenlike state of relaxation. As a result, her coat was always lustrous and silky.

Not long after Trixie became a Koontz, we invited friends to Sunday lunch, already confident that Trixie would be better behaved than I would. Mine is not a high standard of conduct, so her behavior was impressive only because it exceeded mine by a wide margin.

After combing Trixie, we had more tasks—preparing appetizers, arranging flowers, setting the table—than time to accomplish them. We raced this way and that all morning, and as eleven o'clock drew near, our anxiety escalated to panic. A moment after we completed preparations, the doorbell rang.

Our friends found Trixie as delightful as she found them, and the next four hours unfolded so well that Martha Stewart would have pinched our cheeks in approval. Toward the end of lunch, Short Stuff began to bump her nose against my leg and paw at me for attention while we were still at the table. Just in case anyone has ever affectionately referred to Martha Stewart as Short Stuff, let me clarify that I am speaking here of Trixie. This bumping-pawing was uncharacteristic behavior. I told her, "Down," a command I would never have issued to Martha Stewart but one that good Trixie obeyed, lying on the floor beside my dining-room chair. After a few minutes, she sought my attention again, and I said, "Down," and as before she at once obeyed.

After lunch, we adjourned to the living room with coffee, to continue our conversation. Trixie sought my attention and Gerda's more than once. We petted her, rubbed her ears, stroked her chin, but she began to paw at us again, as if she was impatient to play. We denied her in a firm but loving tone of voice. We would play vigorously, but only when our guests had departed.

Finally Trixie stopped seeking play and sat directly in front of the sofa, staring solemnly and intently at me, as if she had recently read a book about mind over matter and hoped, with nothing but focused thought, to levitate me. When I ignored her, she finally left the room for a while and later returned in a less insistent mood.

A few minutes after our guests departed at three thirty, I found a wet blot on the off-white carpet in the family room. Pee. Trixie had gone to the farthest corner, where our guests would not see this faux pas when they passed by the archway, but it was pee nonetheless.

Because Gerda was once a Girl Scout, she learned to be prepared for anything. Trixie had never had an accident that left a "biological stain," as the label on the Nature's

Miracle jar referred to it, but Gerda was ready with a cleanup kit in a canvas carryall. We set to work on the carpet, hoping to address the spot before it became a permanent mark.

Trixie sat at a distance, watching us with what I took to be embarrassment. Her ears drooped, and she hung her head.

Although she was irresistibly cute, I steeled myself to speak to her in a soft but disciplinarian tone. "This is not good," I told her. "Bad. Bad dog. Bad, bad dog. Daddy is disappointed."

She settled onto her belly and crawled across the room as if she were a soldier in a war and my soft words were rifle fire spitting past overhead. She went to a corner as far from the pee as she could get. She lay there with her nose against the baseboard, her back to us, beyond embarrassment, mortified.

As we cleaned the carpet, I kept glancing at Trixie. She looked so pathetic, facing into the corner, that I wanted to go to her and put a hand on her head and tell her all was forgiven. Gerda suggested I do just that, but I said the dog must have been testing us to see if we had the spine to be good masters. We must do the right thing or risk further such challenges.

And then . . . then I remembered what we had been told the day they brought Trixie to us: "If this dog does something wrong, the fault will be yours, not hers." I now understood that when she bumped my leg with her nose and pawed for attention at the dining-room table, when she stared at me as if attempting to levitate or teleport me, she had been telling me that she needed to toilet. With horror, I thought back to how frantic we had been all morning as we prepared for our guests, and I realized that I had forgotten to take her outside for her late-morning pee.

I had failed to follow her schedule, and the pee on the family-room carpet was my fault as surely as if I produced it from my own bladder. As Trixie had been mortified, I was chagrined, which is mortification compounded by disappointment in oneself. I went to her, stroked her, apologized, but she continued to hide her face in the corner.

Gerda had not joined in the verbal disapproval—"Bad dog. Bad, bad dog"—so as usual I was the only hopeless idiot in the room, but she felt so terrible for Trixie that she wanted as much as I did to get us past this moment. "It's her dinnertime. After her kibble, give her a cookie, two cookies. Let's take her down the hill to the park, throw the ball as much as she wants. When we come home, we'll give her a Frosty Paws," which was a frozen treat, ersatz ice cream for dogs.

We did all of that, and through every step of reparations, we kept saying, "Good dog. Good Trixie. Good, good Trixie. Bad Daddy. Gooooood Trixie. Bad, bad Daddy."

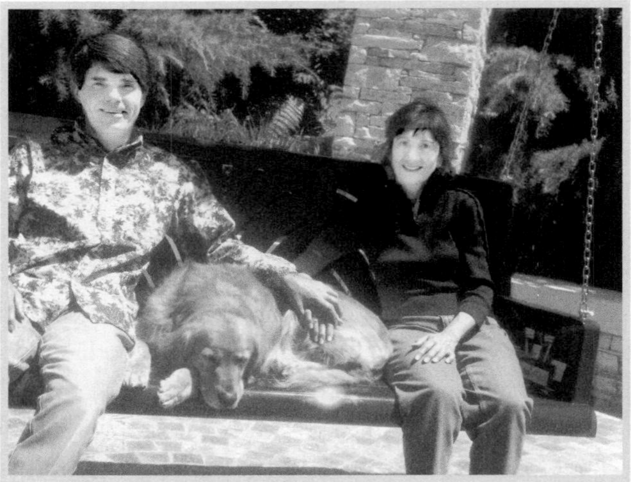

IX

this is where i belong

TWO MONTHS PASSED in a blizzard of tennis balls, which Trixie would retrieve until either I had no more strength to throw them or she dropped from exhaustion.

The shimmer and flash of her golden coat in the sun, the speed with which she pursued her prey, the accuracy of every leap to catch the airborne treasure, the forepaw landing followed by a whip-quick turn the instant the back paws touched the earth . . . She was not just graceful in a physical sense. The more I watched her, the more she seemed to be an embodiment of that greatest of all graces we now and then glimpse, from which we intuitively infer the hand of God, infer the truth that this world's beauty is a gift to sustain the heart, and infer the reality of mercy.

Every time that she came indoors from a walk or a playtime, or from a toileting, we wiped her feet with a damp white cloth to keep dirt out of the house. Some dogs are sensitive about their feet, but Trixie allowed us to manipulate her paws as we wished.

Following a tennis-ball session, however, we used two cloths to scrub not just her paws but also her back legs all the way up to her hocks and the pasterns of her forelimbs past her heelknobs, to remove the grass stains, which were so plentiful that her fur turned bright green. In the chase, when she was too late to leap and snare the ball in descent, she went after it on the bounce with manic glee, sliding dramatically into the catch. If I showed her the green stains on the cloth after scrubbing her, she always sniffed them and then grinned broadly, as if remembering her exuberant play.

When we spent a few days at the beach house, we had no lawn or public park large enough to accommodate a game of throw and retrieve, so we played Trixie's second-favorite sport: *find* the ball. I put her on a sit-stay in one room and went into another, where I hid the tennis ball under a sofa cushion, under an armchair, behind a potted plant, or someplace more cunningly chosen, like high above her head and trapped between a window and a pleated shade. The call "Trixie, find" brought her padding into my room at a near run, head low and nose quivering as she sought the scent of the green nap and rubber.

She never failed to find it, even when I hid it in one room and called her from another, a trick to which she tumbled quicker than I expected. The second time that I hid it in the same room, she went directly to the spot where I had concealed it the first time, to be sure I'd bothered to find an original hiding place.

Balboa Peninsula offered a three-mile boardwalk—actually a paved path—between the oceanfront houses and the beach. Gerda and I often walked it with Trixie. The other walkers, with and without dogs, the in-line skaters weaving through the foot traffic at high speed, the surfers carrying boards to the water, an Indian woman dressed in a colorful sari, a brooding cat curled atop a gatepost, kiting seagulls crying like lost souls: Often during these walks, Trixie would look up at us with a bright expression that said, *Did you see that, wasn't that amazing?*

Trixie inspired me to look at things from a new perspective, made the familiar fresh again, somehow shared with me her recognition of great beauty in mundane scenes, and reawakened in me an awareness of the mystery that is woven into the warp and weft of everything we perceive with our five senses but can *know* only with our hearts. This may be the primary purpose of dogs: to restore our sense of wonder and to help us maintain it, to make us consider that we should trust our intuition as they trust theirs, and to help us realize that a thing known intuitively can be as real as anything known by material experience.

Our first stay at the beach house with Trixie came on the four days of Thanksgiving weekend. On Sunday evening, we returned to our house on the hill—and experienced an unexpected moment of piercing emotion, courtesy of our golden girl.

Whenever we were out with Trixie and came home with packages of any kind, we always let her into the house through the connecting door from the garage, switched on the foyer light, and told her to wait. A minute or two later, arms loaded with grocery bags or mail, we followed her inside and always found her patiently waiting.

Returning at night, that Sunday after Thanksgiving, we followed this routine, but when we entered the house with armfuls of laundry and feast-day leftovers, Trixie was not in the foyer. The rest of the house was dark, and when I called her name, she did not appear out of either the living room or the family room, or out of the dining room.

A sweeping staircase rose from the foyer and turned to meet the open gallery that served the second-floor rooms. At the head of these steps were the double doors to the master suite, one of which stood open, as we had left it.

Carrying a favorite Booda duck in her mouth, Trixie bolted from the dark bedroom, where many of her toys were stored near her dog bed. In a state of great excitement, she hurried down the stairs and raced repeatedly around the foyer, squeak-squeak-squeaking the duck, bounding more than running, capering more than bounding, nothing less than rapturous. We had never previously seen her in such a state of bliss.

Gerda and I stood watching this exhibition with astonishment, at first wondering about the reason for it, but then arriving at the obvious explanation as Trixie's jubilation continued undiminished. Although only three years and two months old, our girl had lived in six places: with her breeder for two months, with her puppy raiser until she was nearly eighteen months, at CCI during the six months that she received advanced training, with Jenna, the young woman she assisted for six months, with her puppy raiser again, while recuperating from elbow surgery, and most recently with us. When we had taken her to the beach house for the holiday, she recognized it as the place where she had met us, *must* have recognized it because she did not rush to explore it as she always did a new place. Throughout that four-day weekend, she expected that we would pass her along to yet new people and that she would be leaving her sixth home for her seventh. When we took her back to our house on the hill, she raced up the stairs to the master suite, found her bed where it should have been, found all her toys as she had left them, and realized that she was not being shipped off to a new place after all.

The running, the bounding, the capering, the squeak-squeak-squeaking merriment was a *celebration* of the recognition that this was still her home and that we were her family forever. We were so touched, we knelt at once on the foyer floor to further reassure her. Trixie came to us, tail lashing, butt wiggling furiously. She dropped the toy duck and licked our hands, though she was not a dog given to much licking. She snuffled against our hands, and gave us that joyful golden smile from which every lover of the breed takes much delight.

Scientists and animal behaviorists have written libraries full of nonsense about the emotions of dogs, suggesting that they do not have emotions as we know them, or that their exhibitions that appear to be emotionally based do not mean what we interpret them to mean in our sentimental determination to see a fellowship between humanity and canines. Like too many specialists in every field, they are educated not out of their ignorance but *into* ignorance, because they are raised to an imagined state of enlightenment—which is actually dogmatism—where they no longer experience the light of intuition and the fierce brightness of common sense. They see the world through cloudy windows of theory and ideology, which obscure reality. This is why most experts in economics never see the financial disaster coming until the wave breaks over them, why most experts in statecraft and military strategy can be undone by an enemy's surprise attack.

As anyone who has ever opened his heart and mind to a dog knows, these creatures have emotions very like our own. The usual arguments against this truth are, by their convoluted nature and by the hidebound materialism that informs them, revealed as sophistry or, worse, as the dogmatic insistence of science that is in fact scientism.

That night, on our return to the house on the hill, Trixie was declaring, *This is where I belong,* and was expressing her joy that at last she had a place in the world from which she would not be taken.

Trixie's sense of place in our family grew, as did her place in our hearts. Later, in a smaller but nonetheless lovely moment, she repeated this declaration in a much different fashion.

We had thrown a party at the beach house at which such a good time was had by all that the last guests did not leave until half past midnight and we did not finish the cleanup until almost two o'clock. We had not come prepared to stay the night and needed to return to the house on the hill.

No dog was ever more people-oriented than Trixie. I believe this was her nature, but her nature had been reinforced by CCI, which must train its assistance dogs to ignore other dogs when on duty with the person that it serves. She met only a few people that she didn't like, and of course she was adored in return. At a party, she always circulated until she dropped.

She had barely enough energy to jump into the back of our SUV. Usually, she would have curled up in the cargo space and snoozed in transit.

Perhaps because we were again at the beach house but now on our way to the place that she considered home, she did not want to be separated from us. As I got behind the wheel and started the engine, Trixie scrambled out of the cargo area, into the backseat, across the console, and onto Gerda's lap. Weighing sixty-two pounds at that time and given the appearance of greater bulk by her thick golden coat, she looked bigger than her mom. She curled up on Gerda, propped her chin on the curve of the door that might be called the windowsill, and sighed with contentment.

This is where I belong, the sigh clearly said, and it so touched Gerda that she would make no effort to dislodge her furry daughter. As we drove home, Trixie began to snore, her breath lightly steaming the side window, safe in loving arms.

Dogs might love a place, as people do, but the only place they love beyond all others is the place where you are. When we left the house on the hill, in Harbor Ridge, home would become wherever we took her.

Once the walls of our new house were framed and the windows set in place, Trixie padded room to room with tail continuously wagging. Visit after visit, her delight was obvious as she capered through the structure, as though she had developed a deep appreciation for the style of Frank Lloyd Wright, which inspired the project.

After months of watching her react with enthusiasm to the place, we suddenly realized what most appealed to her. Our Harbor Ridge house was Victorian, with French windows set well above her head. In the new house, windows in many rooms were instead five feet wide and extended ceiling to floor. When the view mattered, that entire wall of a room was one large-paned window beside another, expansive sweeps of wood-framed glass that brought the outer world into the house. In Harbor Ridge, she could glimpse the outside only through a few French doors. In the new place, she could see nature wherever she went, and this sent her spirit soaring.

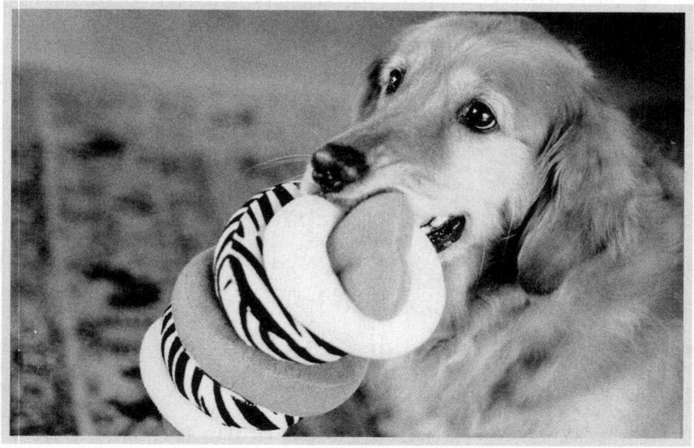

X

please don't send my sweet dog to jail

ON OUR FIRST Christmas together as a married couple, six weeks after the wedding, Gerda and I had too little money to decorate our tree as grandly as we would have liked. Two sets of colored lights, two boxes of cheap ornaments, and a package of aluminum-foil icicles stretched our budget to the breaking point.

We had furnished our entire rented house for a hundred

fifty dollars by seeking bargains at country auctions. This proved to be an effective strategy, but only after we realized we were both raising our hands, bidding against each other, and stopped competing for items we wanted. A sofa bought for three bucks looked handsome after we restrung the springs and reupholstered it with a cheap, attractive material. We attached short legs to an old door, painted it black, and employed it as a Japanese-style dining table. Instead of chairs at the table, we had plump pillows that Gerda stitched together with her sewing machine. They were stuffed with shredded plastic bags—mostly bread bags of soft plastic, so they wouldn't crackle—that our families and their neighbors saved for us, and when we dined, we sat cross-legged on them. We slept on a bizarre combination sofa bed and trundle bed, no more than a foot off the floor.

When she visited us, my mother wept at our poverty. "You're eating on the *floor,*" she said with great distress, emphasizing the last word of each sentence, as though reciting an official litany of misery. "You're sleeping on the *floor.* You don't have an *oven.* You don't have a *TV. You're eating on the FLOOR.*" She loved us. She wanted the best for us. My mother had lived her entire married life not knowing if she would have a roof over her head tomorrow, yet she reacted to our humble but happy home as if we were festering in a cardboard shanty in the slums of Calcutta.

Our first Christmas tree did not dazzle. There were not piles of gifts stacked beneath it. But we were together, we no longer stood separate and alone in the world, we owned a nice electric hot plate, we didn't waste time watching TV because we didn't have one to watch, and if we fell out of bed in the night, we couldn't drop far enough to hurt ourselves. At twilight on Christmas Eve, snow began to spiral down in silver-dollar flakes, and we went for a walk in an evening as magical as any in Narnia.

Thirty-two years later, as our first Christmas with Trixie approached, we anticipated the holiday with as much pleasure as we felt in that distant December. With the success of my books, Gerda and I had long been purchasing art and antiques that we both admired; we thought of those things as gifts to ourselves, and years earlier, we stopped exchanging Christmas presents with each other because they seemed superfluous. Now we had a special dog to spoil. Although we might not be able to explain Santa Claus to her, we were eager to play the role.

We bought plush toys, tug toys, toss toys, more plush toys, plush toys that were also tug toys, balls that squeaked, balls that did not squeak, and a ball with an inner light that flashed when it rolled. We wrapped these gifts in boxes to disguise their size and shape, as though Trixie would be more surprised and delighted by a Frisbee that came out of a big rectangular box than by one that came out of a flat, square, Frisbee-shaped package.

We intended to open her gifts on Christmas Eve, after dinner, which is the time Gerda and I had exchanged presents in the days when we still shopped for each other. Half an hour before, I took Trixie upstairs for a play session that, with my usual athletic grace, I managed to transform into a medical emergency.

As you may recall, early in her life with us, in a strangely destructive mood not characteristic of her, Trixie found where we kept the stepstool, dragged it upstairs, positioned it below an oil painting that Gerda particularly liked, climbed the stool, and hit the painting with a Kong toy. Subsequently, we were not allowed to have a stepstool in the long upstairs hallway, and I couldn't throw a tennis ball for Short Stuff to chase; I could only roll the ball with a velocity-generating snap of the wrist.

We had always engaged in this game with me on my knees, down at Trixie's level, largely because goldens are *soooooo* much cuter seen from their perspective than from above. Over time, the play evolved until it was as much about me trying to fake her out as it was about me rolling the ball and her chasing it. Exceedingly quick, she could sometimes snatch the ball as it zoomed by her, eliminating the need to sprint after it for the length of the hall. But with a young dog, as with children, one purpose of play is to tire the pup enough so you'll be able to do something *you* want to do for at least part of the evening. And at three, our girl was still in some ways a pup.

I developed a repertoire of fake-out moves to keep Trixie unsure of whether I would roll the ball past her port side or her starboard side. I would lean toward her port and tense my rolling arm, so she would lean toward port, all of this very quick, and then I would lean toward her starboard, so she would lean toward starboard, and then I would start to lean toward her port again, but as she shifted her weight to that side, I would snap the ball past her starboard after all. Eventually, I had a million variations of this. Now and then, I was able to roll the ball between her forepaws and between her back legs, which always freaked her out, so that she sprang off the floor and executed an airborne turn.

In addition, I distracted Trixie from watching my ball hand by making funny noises, by throwing a wadded Kleenex at her just before rolling the ball, by a variety of spastic movements that simulated the effects of electrocution, by revealing a piece of kibble and dropping it on the carpet, and by casting my voice as best I could to meow like a seductive cat. Face wrenched by fear, I pointed overhead at nonexistent pterodactyls, which often worked because, in spite of her intelligence and her CCI education, Trixie did not pay attention in her paleontology classes and did not have a clear understanding of what forms of life existed in previous geologic periods but not in our own.

Sometimes, she was so wired that as the ball went past her, she pounced on it again and again, as lightning-quick as a starving gecko on a tasty cricket. On those occasions, to be able to fake her out, I needed to come closer to her than three feet, so that when I snapped the ball, my hand was already past her front legs. Perhaps you, dear reader, are perspicacious enough to understand the risk of this move and the inevitable bloody consequences. I am only a writer of novels, however, and do not possess a sufficient knowledge of physics and hand/eye-coordination dynamics to be able to foresee the consequences of every dumb move I make.

Executing this particular dumb move, I faked to Trixie's port, to starboard, to port, to port, to port, then actually snapped it past her port side as she mistakenly anticipated a last switch to starboard. As the ball left my right hand, Trixie at once realized her mistake and whipped her head around. My open hand was rising off the floor, her open mouth was coming around in the hope of snatching the ball, which was off and rolling, and one of her long upper canines tore through the meaty part of my palm.

The radial artery crosses the palm of the human hand. At that point of its transit of the arm, it's not one of those deliciously large arteries that would interest Dracula, but it keeps a lot of capillaries generously supplied. Trixie might have nicked the artery, but she definitely tore through a bunch of capillaries. Blood flew in a bright spray, and my golden girl raced after the ball, unaware of what had happened.

Using my left hand to pinch the laceration shut, trying to spill as little blood as possible, both because the carpet was off-white and because I am philosophically opposed to allowing my blood to leave my body, I hurried to the nearest bathroom, which was off Gerda's office, snatched the hand towel from the rack, and bound up my right hand.

Trixie returned with the ball, which she dropped at my feet, eager to continue playing. I said, "Not now, sweetie. I think a pterodactyl bit me."

As she followed me out of Gerda's office and into the upstairs hall, she sniffed at the blood on the carpet but made no effort to lick any of it. I would like to think her restraint arose from the fact that this was her beloved dad's blood, not because it had a tainted odor.

Downstairs, Gerda prepared for the much-anticipated Trixie's-first-Christmas-as-a-Koontz, gift-opening lollapalooza. There would be wine and cheese and nuts for us, little cookies for Trixie, and now plenty of blood for everyone.

Managing not to scream like a little girl, I located Gerda in the kitchen, explained what had happened, and asked her to drive me to the hospital. We left Trixie alone, sternly admonishing her not to open any gifts in our absence and to leave the stepstool in the closet where it belonged.

Even with minimal respect for speed limits and stop signs, and even though the streets were nearly deserted on Christmas Eve, we needed fifteen minutes to reach the best hospital in the area. I will admit having a prejudice against hospitals that, though nearer, have a high kill rate.

By the time we walked into the emergency room, the towel in which I had wrapped my right hand was so saturated with blood, you couldn't discern that it had once been white. Nevertheless, we were directed to the registration desk, where Gerda and I sat opposite a pleasant young woman who would either arrange for my treatment or would transfer me to the boatman who would pole me across the River Styx, depending on how long we needed to fill out all the paperwork.

She asked me what had happened, and I explained, and she said, "Oh, a dog bite."

"No, no," I corrected. "She didn't bite me. It was an accident. We were playing, and it was entirely my fault."

In a crisis, Gerda is a rock, so even before the receptionist had asked for the insurance card, driver's license, street address, and proof of membership in the human species, she had all the necessary cards on the desk.

Glancing at my insurance card, the young woman said, "Oh, you have the same name as the writer."

When I acknowledged that I shared not only the writer's name but his brain and his wardrobe, and noted that I was here with his wife, the receptionist was delighted to meet me. Her favorite book, she declared, was *Watchers,* though she also loved *Intensity.* As she filled out the forms, she repeatedly paused to ask me why none of the films based on my work resembled the books from which they were adapted (because they're all blithering idiots in Hollywood), why I write so many more women in lead roles in my books than do most male writers (because I've met so many interesting women and married a great one), would I ever write a sequel to *Watchers* (if you can't top the original story, it doesn't need a sequel), and what scares Dean Koontz (the possibility of bleeding to death).

The towel wrapping my hand became so saturated that it dripped blood on the floor.

You might think that I became impatient with the receptionist, but I did not, for three good reasons. One, she liked my books, and although I won't die for people who like my books, I will happily suffer for them. Two, this woman had no way of knowing that I am philosophically opposed to allowing my blood to leave my body. Three, if I'd been the receptionist, and if John D. MacDonald, the writer, had hobbled to me, holding his severed foot in his hands, I would have had a thousand questions for him and might even have asked him to wait while I ran home and got some of his books for him to sign.

Soon, I settled into a wheelchair, and a nurse rolled me out of the waiting room and into the ER proper. I told Gerda to call Trixie and tell her I was going to be all right, and Gerda agreed that she would.

The nurse pushing the wheelchair was also a reader of mine. She said she had read everything I'd written and needed another book, and she asked if I would ever stop writing.

"Not if I live," I promised.

The medical system was in gear now, moving right along. A minute later, I was in an ER bed, surrounded by a privacy curtain, listening to someone sobbing at the farther end of the room.

A young doctor came through the curtain with the flair of a magician. He was handsome enough to join the cast of the television show *ER,* so I knew he must be a highly competent physician.

Indicating the soaked towel that bound my hand, he said, "That's a lot of blood."

"Is it really?" I asked. "I thought I might be overreacting to it since it's, you know, *my* blood."

As he unwound the towel, he asked what had happened, and I told him about the fake-out maneuver in the roll-the-ball game that had gone so very wrong.

"Oh," he said, "a dog bite. I'll have to report a dog bite to Newport Beach Animal Control."

I hastened to correct him, to explain that it was an accident, and to describe again how it had occurred.

"Even so," he said, "if there was a dog involved, the law requires me to report it as a bite. What's the dog's name?"

Frantically considering whether to lie to him and give a false dog name, I did not immediately reply.

When he saw the gash in my palm, he said, "This is a rather deep wound. We need to clean it out and look in there. It'll need eight stitches, maybe ten. What did you say the dog's name was?"

If I gave him a fake name—say, Lulu—then I would have to buy another dog and name it Lulu and turn it over to the animal-control officers when they came to our house in riot helmets and bulletproof vests, toting tear gas and Uzis. Lulu would be innocent, she wouldn't know why she was being booked for assault, and when she was sitting in the dog equivalent of Alcatraz, I would be sleepless with guilt for railroading her.

"Her name is Trixie," I said. "Listen, would a dog named Trixie ever bite anyone? She's a good, good dog. She's a golden retriever. She probably wouldn't even bite a burglar if he was beating me with a shovel."

As we had been conversing, he had also been requesting from a nurse the tools and materials he would need to clean and close the wound. Now she wheeled in a stainless-steel cart bearing a collection of instruments that would have thrilled Hannibal Lecter.

Over the years, a few dentists, a periodontist, an endodontist, a gastroenterologist, and two internists have told me that I have a very high pain threshold. Because I didn't want to be anesthetized, I once endured, without Novocain or any painkillers, the three-hour extraction of a tooth with roots fused to the jawbone.

Now the handsome young doctor, who wanted to send my Trixie to the slammer, told me, "Evidently, you have an unusually high pain threshold."

"I guess that's a good thing," I said, "though I still try to avoid situations that involve pain."

"I'm going to numb your hand anyway, so this won't hurt at all. Is Trixie current with all her shots?"

"Yes," I said. "Rabies, *Bordetella*, corona, measles, mumps, the black plague, the virus that's always turning people into flesh-eating zombies in the movies, all that stuff, everything, up-to-date."

"Who's her vet?"

I told him, and he knew who Dr. Whitaker and Dr. Lyle were. I asked, "What'll animal control do when they get this report?"

"I can't say. I don't know their procedures. I just know what I'm supposed to do in a dog-bite case."

Focused on his work, he remained silent for a long

time as he meticulously cleaned the wound, examined it, stopped the bleeding, and finally closed it.

Although I was worried about Trixie, I was grateful that unlike the receptionist and the nurse, the doctor had made no reference to my books and was unaware that I was a well-known writer. I did not intend to try to bribe him, and I didn't think a death threat would be taken seriously, so when I wept and begged him to have mercy on my four-legged daughter, I could do so with confidence that the story of my shameless groveling and my plea for special treatment would not end up on a tabloid TV show.

As he finished repairing my hand, the doctor said, "So, in the future, maybe you should have more cats in your books and fewer dogs."

After thanking him for his good work, I made one last pitch for him to join me in a conspiracy against the forces of law and order run amok. "Trixie was a CCI assistance dog, she retired young because of elbow surgery, she's as sweet as a dog can be, and I hate the idea that she's going to have a police record. You know, it *is* Christmas Eve."

He smiled, shook his head, gave me a prescription, instructions, and a date for the removal of the stitches.

Gerda drove us home, and Trixie greeted us with much love, which we repaid with interest.

Using a terrific spot remover, we quickly cleaned up all the blood on the carpet, and then decided to present Trixie's gifts to her, as planned, though later than expected. We were determined not to let her know that the terrible hammer of the law might come down on her at any time.

No child ever received gifts with more excitement and delight than Trixie did. The rustle of tissue paper in particular caused her to wriggle with anticipation. We played a little with each toy, then unwrapped the next one, encouraging her to sniff and paw at every package.

Before we retired for the night, we disposed of all the torn wrappings and ribbons and boxes, and we lined up the twenty-one unwrapped gifts on the L-shaped family-room sectional.

Every morning since she had been with us, Trixie followed the same routine. When we came out of the bedroom with her to take her on her first walk of the day, she raced down the back stairs and turned left into the kitchen, padding straight to the pantry, where her kibble was stored in a large airtight can.

On this first Christmas morning as a Koontz, however, she descended the back stairs with even greater haste than usual and turned right, not toward the kitchen but into the family room. As we watched, she went from one gift to the next, smelling each of the twenty-one, as if astonished to find that the previous evening had not been a dream and that all these toys were in fact hers. When she checked out the twenty-first and then looked at us, her grin was endearing.

I believe the ER doctor filed the report with animal

control, as required, but I suspect he might have added some exculpatory comments. We never received a call from the authorities, and Trixie gamboled through the rest of her years, happily unaware that her spotless reputation had been at risk because of her dad's lack of athletic prowess.

XI
things that go boom

OUR FIRST JULY Fourth with Trixie, we lived in Harbor Ridge, where we enjoyed a panoramic view of Newport Beach all the way to the sea, northwest to Long Beach, and north to the San Bernardino Mountains. On a clear Independence Day evening, we could see four or five major fireworks displays, some nearby and others at a distance.

Generally speaking, dogs aren't cool with fireworks. The pretty patterns of color and light don't impress them, but the boom-bang-crackle-crash makes them nuts. Most memoirs about dogs have a chapter detailing how Fido, left alone on a July Fourth evening or during a big thunderstorm, did more damage to the house than would have a runaway logging truck.

In this matter, as in so many others, Trixie behaved differently from our expectations. When the fireworks started, we watched them from an upper-floor balcony, and our golden girl stood with us, intrigued. She even put her head between two of the balusters to have a better view of the spectacle. Her tail wagged when the sky filled with girandoles, palm trees, magnesium peonies, and other types of fireworks that at most hissed or crackled but did not boom. During the louder flash-bangs, her tail stopped wagging and she stiffened slightly, but she didn't tremble or whimper.

Over time, she lost enthusiasm for skyrockets and Roman candles, but never became terrified of them. She trembled when the loud ones went off, but cuddling was sufficient to soothe her.

In southern California, we seldom experience pyrotechnic storms. Whether light or heavy, rain comes with subtropical languor. Thunder and lightning occur on average no more than once a year, though two or three years can pass without such a spectacle.

When she was younger, Trixie grew mildly irritated by thunder, but as she aged, she developed a fear of violent storms. I think it was less the noise than the combination of noise and night, because when once we had a daytime downpour with a lot of sky drumming, she was unnerved but not fearful, and she even stood at a big window to study the day, as if to determine the source of the sound.

One evening, however, we were hammered by the worst thunderstorm I've ever known. Even in the mountains of Pennsylvania, where rain seldom comes *without* cannons in the heavens, I never heard such cacophony. The deluge started before ten o'clock in the evening with a detonation that sounded as if the cosmos might be collapsing.

Gerda and I had gone to bed but were not yet asleep, and we sat up, startled, mistaking the thunder for another kind of explosion, until the sudden roar of rain followed it. Trixie shot off her bed and paced the room, agitated.

We switched on a lamp. A soft light sometimes soothed our girl.

Peals of thunder continued, low rolling rumbles suggestive of ominous war machines conquering territory in the distance, punctuated by tremendous cracks and crashes so vehement that the foundations of the world seemed to be under assault and giving way.

Trixie did not whine or growl. She did not shiver with fear. But she paced restlessly around the bedroom. Every time an exceptionally hard clap of thunder chased blast waves that vibrated in the window glass and trembled the walls, she went still and waited expectantly for some terrible consequence of the sound—then continued to pace.

We tried to get her to jump on the bed with us, but she

wanted to keep moving, alert for some threat of which the thunder warned. When after a while the loud detonations stopped and there were only long low grumbles like some huge beast softly growling in its sleep, she returned to her bed but remained alert and nervous.

Either a series of storm cells harried the night or the same storm kept circling back to us. Each time it seemed that the rumbling sky would settle into silence, the booming began again, as bad or worse than the previous round of detonations.

Finally, after midnight, Trixie decided that being closer to her family was better than ceaselessly roaming, and she jumped onto the bed with us. We encouraged her to cuddle, but she sat at the foot of the mattress, facing the windows, which were covered by roll-down wood shutters.

The storm seemed about to crescendo, but the escalating tumult roared for hours. As the night dragged on, Trixie turned her back to the windows and hour by hour, always panting with anxiety, she inched up the bed, between Gerda and me. Flat on our backs, we reached up to scratch her chest, to touch her face, to stroke her sides, and once in a while she would lower her head to lick one of our hands or to rub her cold nose against our fingers in gratitude for our presence. We could not induce her to lie down, perhaps because she thought that she would be vulnerable if not standing or at least sitting. Just after four o'clock, she traveled as far as she could, her chest against the headboard, her nose against the wall.

If the thunder had not kept Gerda and me awake,

Trixie's fear and panting would have made sleep impossible. We had work that needed to be done when morning came, appointments to be kept; we were going to be shambling through our meetings as if we were the walking dead.

At four thirty, the sky quieted at last. Exhausted, Trixie did not lie down so much as collapse on the bed, her head on Gerda's pillow, her fluffy butt in my face. Instantly, she began to snore.

We had to get up at six o'clock, and we did not have a dog's ability to switch off like a lamp. We knew that we would lie awake until the alarm clock rang.

Throughout the long night, Gerda and I had said little to each other, trying to remain sleep-ready in case the thunder stopped and the panting dog grew quiet. Now, with Trixie snoring between our heads, Gerda said, "I'm going to be a wreck all day . . . but I wouldn't trade this experience for the world."

I knew exactly what she meant. We had never previously needed to gentle our girl through such a long seizure of anxiety. Being there for her and knowing that she took courage from us, we fulfilled the promise that dog lovers make to their dogs—*I will always love you and bring you safely through troubled times*—and little in life is as satisfying as keeping promises.

XII

things that go bump in the night

TRIXIE HAD BEEN with us a year when she did something nearly as mystifying as her reaction when I told her that I knew she was an angel posing as a dog.

Gerda and I were sitting up in bed, reading, about ready to turn off the lights and go to sleep.

Trixie got up from her bed to get a drink. On her way back to the corner, she performed one of those cute-as-it-gets stretches in which her rump raised high, the rest of her sloped down toward the floor, her legs thrust straight out in front of her, and her toes spread wide as if all the weariness in her muscles were pouring forward through her body and draining out through her forepaws.

No sooner had she settled down than she leaped up again, ran past our bed, and vanished through the open door into the upstairs hall.

Because we had looked up from our books to watch Trixie stretch, our attention remained on her when she hurriedly split. She had never raced off like this before, and we both thought, *Intruder.*

I had set the perimeter alarm prior to settling down to read, but perhaps someone had already been in the house when I activated the system. Such an unlikely event had happened a couple of years earlier, before we had Trixie.

One night, we went out for dinner and forgot to arm the security system. When we came home, we entered from the garage, went straight up the main stairs to the master suite, locked the door behind us, and set the alarm to night mode, which engaged all doors and windows but also motion detectors in the hallways. We didn't know an intruder was in the house, lurking in a second-floor study when we returned.

The computerized voice of the alarm announced any change in conditions by way of the house music-system speakers. Therefore, the trespasser in the study knew he was trapped in that space by the motion detector in the hallway, which would trigger a siren and call the police with a recorded message if he moved through its field of observation. Apparently, he settled down to wait and think.

Feeling as safe as Pooh and Tigger in the most benign district of their entirely comfortable forest, Gerda and I got ready for bed, sat up reading for an hour or two, and then went to sleep. At two in the morning, the alarm screamed, and the Hal-9000 voice informed us that someone had opened the study window.

Because that window was on the second floor, fifteen feet above the walkway along the south side of the house, reachable from outside only with a ladder, we assumed the alarm must be false. After turning off the security system, I went to the study to check for corrosion of the contact points between window and sill—and discovered the window open.

Yikes. I hurried back to the master bedroom, armed myself, and returned cautiously to the study and peered out of the open window. No ladder. Someone had opened the window to flee the house, not to invade. He had dropped onto a rain-shelter roof over a first-floor side door directly below, cracking a couple of cedar shingles, and from there he had jumped to the walkway.

After brooding on his situation, the trapped intruder had most likely decided that the second-floor windows might not be tied into the alarm system. Many people save money by not wiring hard-to-reach windows.

Fortunately, the folks from whom we bought the house were paranoid enough to wire even those openings that could be reached only by the ape from Edgar Allan Poe's *Murders in the Rue Morgue*. Otherwise, our uninvited guest might have escaped without anyone knowing that he'd been there. When the window was found open, I or Gerda would have assumed that the other had left it that way, for ventilation.

Now, two years later, when Trixie sprang off her bed and raced into the upstairs hall, we wondered if the intruder had returned or perhaps had recommended our accommodations to a criminal pal. Trixie neither growled nor barked, but then she rarely did either, and it was possible that she hoped the intruder might have a cookie or a tennis ball.

When I followed her into the hall, I found her standing near the door to Gerda's office. She was gazing up, as though making eye contact with someone about my height, smiling and wagging her tail.

I said, "Trixie, what's happening?"

Ignoring me, still appearing to be attentive to someone I could not see, she padded out of the hallway and into Gerda's dark office.

Even if Trixie might be hesitant to bark at a burglar, her sudden appearance would have startled a yelp out of him if he'd been in Gerda's sanctum. I followed the dog across the threshold and switched on the light.

She stood at a far corner of Gerda's desk, still peering up at something, bright-eyed and engaged. Her tail swished, swished.

A tail is a communications device, a compensation for

not having the capacity for language. Its position and its motion—or lack of motion—can convey a dog's mood and intentions. With its tail, a dog talks to other dogs, to people, to cats, to all manner of creatures.

Rarely if ever does a dog wag its tail at an inanimate object. Even the dumbest dog knows the difference between inanimate objects and living beings that might be able to read what it is saying in tail speak.

Trixie returned around Gerda's desk, still looking up as if the invisible man had stepped out of a movie and into our home. She remained oblivious of me, responding not at all when I spoke her name and called her to me.

In the hall again, she paused, grinning up at her make-believe friend. She did a little dance of delight before proceeding next into the office in which Linda worked.

Here, we went through a repeat of the performance in Gerda's office, as if Short Stuff were following a visitor on a tour of the premises.

By the time Trix and I—and whoever—returned to the hallway, Gerda had come out of the master suite to see what was happening. Trixie seemed as unaware of Gerda as she continued to be of me.

After her paws pranced in place, performing another little dance of delight, our girl proceeded along the hallway to my office. There, we watched as she seemed to accompany someone around the room.

I am not a guy who sees ghosts or ever expects to see one. If I need a good scare to get my blood circulating, I just switch on the evening news and see what the latest batch of insane politicians is up to.

I would later publish a series of books about a young man named Odd Thomas, who sees the spirits of the lingering dead. But this peculiar moment with Trixie occurred long before that, when ghost stories were not yet on my agenda.

After leaving my office, in the hallway once more, Trixie stood gazing up at someone about six feet tall, her tail in motion. Then her wagging slowly diminished, stopped. She lowered her head, shook herself, and surveyed her surroundings, at last noticing us. She chuffed and grinned as if to say, *Cool, huh?* Then she trotted back to the master suite, curled in her bed, and fell asleep.

As I went room to room, turning off lights, I wondered about the history of our house, whether anyone had died in it. Even if someone had hung himself from the foyer chandelier, I couldn't believe that he would be haunting the place. What's believable and right in a work of allegorical fiction isn't easily embraced in real life by a person of reason. I decided not to worry about it when I realized that my good dog's tail had been wagging vigorously throughout her encounter; she had been enchanted by what she saw, and she wouldn't be enchanted by a spirit with malevolent intentions.

A couple of friends have suggested that Trixie might have been following a moth in flight or some small winged insect that I didn't notice. As lame as that explanation is,

I considered it. But given how long the episode lasted and how many well-lighted rooms were on the tour, no moth or its equivalent could have escaped my attention.

Besides, Trixie never before or after that event was lured into the pursuit of any insect other than a few fine butterflies on summer days. And those butterfly chases were frisky, leaping exercises in doggy exuberance, nothing like the leisurely walk-around of the second floor that evening.

A number of people have told me stories about their dogs seeming to see things that humans can't see, although none of their accounts were similar to mine. I do believe Trixie saw *something* that she found enchanting and that remained beyond my ken. I'll never know what it might have been—unless in some other plane of existence I am reunited with her one day, and in that new world, she can talk.

During the almost eight additional years that we were fortunate enough to have Trixie, she never repeated that performance, and never exhibited any other kind of fey behavior. Nonetheless, I believe the moment was meaningful, revealing a special quality that cannot be easily defined but that was central to this dog's uniqueness.

XIII

a nose for trouble

EVEN SERIAL KILLERS have dogs they love and that return their affection, though it's difficult to imagine John Wayne Gacy knitting a sweater for a Chihuahua or Jeffrey Dahmer taking time away from his collection of severed heads to frolic in the park with a Labradoodle.

Perhaps Stalin's dogs had to love him or otherwise be shipped to a Siberian forced-labor camp, but no doubt they would have loved him without the threat of a life sentence to a Gulag. Consequently, we are not on solid ground if we insist that dogs are better judges of character than are human beings.

Yet I've heard people make this claim many times. And we have all seen movies in which only the dog recognizes that the new babysitter is a bug-eating psychopath or that the genial neighbor in the cardigan has been replaced by a shape-changing alien with an appetite for human sweetbreads.

Nevertheless, over time I learned that Trixie was an uncannily good judge of character with both humans and canines. While it's true that she was people-oriented and liked nearly everyone she met to one degree or another, she seemed indifferent to about 10 percent of the people she encountered. She was not wary of or hostile to that fraction of humanity; she simply had little or no interest in them.

With the other 90 percent, her greeting always consisted of at minimum a grin and a wagging tail. The faster the tail moved, the more she approved of the person before her. About half the time, she raised her right forelimb and gently pawed at a new acquaintance as if to say, *I'm here, see me, I like you, come down here where we can sniff each other's face.* This was a higher degree of approval than merely a grin and a wag. She expressed total acceptance by collapsing as if her legs had turned to rubber, rolling onto her back, and baring her tummy for her new friend's admiration and attention.

•

The longer Trix was with us, the more I realized that the people to whom she presented her belly were the true friends with whom I, too, could leave myself entirely vulnerable without fear of attack. And those about whom she had mild reservations were also those whom I liked very much but felt I didn't entirely know—although in my case, I would not be better able to discern the fine points of their character by sniffing their faces.

People whom I found to be cold or false, or in some other way off-putting, were without exception in the 10 percent toward whom Trixie remained indifferent. When these were individuals whom I had met previously, the argument could be made that from a score of subtle telltales in my demeanor and behavior, Trixie instantly read my opinion of the person and adopted it as her own. Dogs study us their whole lives and learn the meaning of our tiniest changes of expression and voice inflection. But when I met someone for the first time, Trixie's opinion and mine also matched, though she instantly identified the troubling individuals as worthy only of indifference, while I needed longer to make the same judgment.

Only once did Trixie react so negatively to someone that she refused even to allow that person to touch her. I should have taken our golden girl's warning seriously.

To protect the guilty, I will not indicate that person's gender or occupation, and will use only the name X.

I knew X for the better part of a decade but only through a business relationship and from a distance. A couple of years earlier, before we were blessed with Trixie,

X came to southern California with Y and Z, two people who worked for the company that employed X, and although they were not traveling on business related to us, Gerda and I took them all to dinner. The evening was not filled with the scintillating conversation and hilarity that might have made me want to say, "Let's take turns flying across country once a week and do this every Friday night for the rest of our lives," but we had a pleasant time.

When Trixie came to us, she was welcomed not merely as a pet; she participated in every aspect of our lives, including taking a role in my relationship with my most faithful readers. Those who live in the United States and write to me by snail mail have long received a twelve-page newsletter—*Useless News*—that informs them of forthcoming books but is largely about having fun, reprinting humorous pieces I've written. We began using photos of Trixie in the newsletter, adding funny captions. She wrote reviews of my forthcoming books, solemnly swearing that her praise could not be bought for cookies. Whenever a book failed to include a dog in at least a minor role, she gave it less than a five-star rating. I had so much fun creating Trixie's singular manner of expression that eventually she would publish successful books "edited by" or "as told to" Dean Koontz.

As someone with whom I did business and as someone who claimed to read and like my books, X received *Useless News* and became a fan of Trixie. Eventually, X returned to California on a business trip, and we arranged a visit at the house before we went to lunch.

Usually, on hearing the chimes, Trixie bolted to the front door, eager to see who had come calling. This time, she hurried into the foyer as usual, but as I opened the door, she turned and scampered away so fast that X failed to get a glimpse of her.

I didn't think much about this abrupt retreat. Perhaps she had heard someone open the pantry door in the kitchen, where her can of kibble was kept. She always assumed that no one could have any other purpose for entering the pantry except to get food for her.

I welcomed X into the living room, we chatted for a bit, and then I called upstairs to Linda to find out if Trixie was with her. Trix indeed had retreated to that office, and I asked Linda to bring her down to the living room.

Trixie descended the front stairs warily, but remained in the foyer while Linda came through the living room archway to say hello to X. She tried to return upstairs with Linda, but I said, "Trixie, here," and she wouldn't disobey me. She stepped hesitantly to the archway, her tail held low.

Leaning forward in an armchair, X said, "Here, cutie, come give me a kiss."

After a quick glance toward our visitor, Trixie refused to look at X again, as if by doing so she would risk being turned to stone. As X continued to wheedle, Trixie's ears seemed to droop as if all the cartilage had melted out of them, and she hung her head as she might have if she expected at any moment to be beaten.

When she finally ventured into the living room, she slunk to me, where I sat on a sofa, and pressed up against my leg, as though for reassurance. If a large coffee table hadn't stood between me and X, I don't believe Trixie would have ventured out of the foyer.

Having told X that the Trickster was people-loving, as friendly as any canine who ever lived, so friendly that she made Lassie seem like a savage attack dog, I found our girl's behavior a little bit embarrassing. In retrospect, perhaps this development should have made me nervous. But I had known X for years by telephone, even if this was only our second face-to-face encounter. I had no reason to think that I was dealing with an individual whose appearance and whose reality were as different as a rose is different from a garlic bulb.

I suggested to X that Trixie must not be feeling well, and I took her upstairs to Gerda. Thereafter, I drove X to lunch.

At the restaurant, after ordering but before we had been served more than iced tea, X said, "After lunch, I want to take a tour of your beach house."

This statement struck me as somewhat forward, especially because it was delivered as a desire, almost as a demand, rather than as a request. Furthermore, X knew that I was on a deadline, working long days, and that to make up for the couple of hours we were taking for lunch,

I would have to stay at the keyboard later into the night than usual.

Referring again to that deadline, I suggested that perhaps we could tour the beach house the next time X was on the West Coast.

"Just give me the address, directions, and the key," X said, "and I'll have a look at it on my own this afternoon."

Faintly but unmistakably, in my mind's ear, I began to hear the shrieking violins that accompanied every slashing of the knife in *Psycho*.

"Well," I lied, "today isn't a good day anyway, because the exterminator tented the house for termites. You can't get inside."

We talked about termites for a while, and X revealed no peculiar thoughts about them or about insects of any kind, and then we moved on to the subject of mold and dry rot, which are also problems when you have a house on the water in a warm climate, and somehow we went from dry rot to chatting about recent movies. Minute by minute, the give-me-the-keys-to-your-house-I-want-to-snoop-through-your-closets request seemed less real, as if I must have misunderstood, and the X who had asked for the keys, Bizarro X, seemed to have been someone I imagined.

After our food was served and as we began to eat, X said, "I'm going to come stay at your beach house for a few weeks this summer."

The shrieking violins returned, and suddenly my food tasted like something termites might have gnawed on. Smiling as if I saw nothing strange in X's announcement, I said, "Oh, well, you know, we don't rent the place out, it's not an income-producing property."

"Yes, I know," said X, "that's what'll make it such a special vacation, like staying in a wonderful home, not like a hotel."

Disquieted by the presence of a sharp knife beside X's plate, I tried to convince myself that this person must be pulling my chain, having a laugh at my expense. I might have embraced that notion if X's eyes had not become as feverish as those of a malaria victim tormented by hallucinations. X stared across the table at me as Rasputin must have stared when he mesmerized the czar. Although I was reluctant to meet that intense gaze, breaking eye contact might be read as a weakness.

"Don't worry," X said, "I won't wreck the place."

Of course I knew at once the place would be thoroughly wrecked.

"There must be lots of interesting people to meet in a town like Newport," X continued, "all the surfers, beach bums, and everything, but I'll keep the parties down to one a week."

"Well," I said, "beach properties are pretty close together, and our neighbors don't like parties."

"It's your property," said X, "they can't make rules for you."

"Ordinarily," I heard myself saying, "I would agree with

you, but our neighbors are crazy skinheads, total gun nuts, they sit on their back patio with assault rifles on their laps, bandoliers of ammunition, you don't want to push them."

X regarded me as I had regarded X: as if I were of questionable sanity.

Instead of continuing to meet craziness with craziness, I said, "Well, as soon as you decide when you'd like to come, let me know the dates, and we'll work it out."

I had no more intention of accommodating X for a three-week vacation than I had of stabling a herd of Aegean horses in the beach house.

Evidently, I sounded sincere, because X said, "Great. It'll be a lot of fun. You and Gerda will be invited to the parties, of course."

"Cool," I said.

For the remainder of lunch, we talked about this and that, as if neither of us belonged in an asylum, and Bizarro X appeared now and then only as an occasional facial expression that didn't comport with what X was saying. Although telling a funny story, X glowered as if recounting a harrowing encounter with a rabid cat, while a dissertation on the threat of global warming was delivered with a sunny smile.

After surviving lunch and the drive home, when I could easily have been overpowered and strangled with a wire garrote in traffic, I was relieved when X did not suggest staying for dinner and then for the rest of my life. I waved at X's departing rental car as if forlornly bidding adieu to a friend whose absence would make my world a grim, gray place.

A few days later, having returned to the East Coast, X called to give Linda five names to add to our free-book list. Each time a new novel of mine is published, I send inscribed copies to approximately 250 family members and friends, as a way of saying that I'm thinking of them and that my life has been brightened by knowing them over all these years, and another fifty to people who, like X, have been helpful on the business side of my life. The five names provided by X were, of course, strangers to me.

A few days later, X called to give us another five names to add to the free-book list. The following week, X called to say that none of those ten people had yet received their inscribed books, so we might want to resend, this time by Federal Express. A couple of days later, X phoned to leave the name and number of an acquaintance—let's say the name was Q—who had recently been through a bad divorce and needed a shoulder to cry on. X felt that no shoulder in the world would better console Q than that of her favorite author.

Although a time had existed when I personally took calls from X, that time was past. Usually, we had reason to talk four times a year, but X started calling twice a week. Linda fielded all of this with her customary courtesy and patience, but X soon demanded to talk to me—and started ringing before Linda arrived for work or when she might be at lunch, hoping I would be alone and answering my office phone. Being sent to voice mail offended X. We were, after all, going to be partying together next summer, hanging out with a bunch of beach bums and radical dudes, having the best time of our lives.

Without giving the reason, I severed my business relationship with the company that employed X, after which we had no reason to talk. Nonetheless, the calls continued for a couple of years—as did demands for free books to be sent to people who were delighted to have met my best friend, X, and were further delighted to hear that they would never again have to *buy* my novels.

When I had let X into our house that fateful day, Trixie took one whiff before the door was half open, probably did not even get a glimpse of this person, but understood *at once* that a deranged individual loomed at the threshold. She scampered away to hide and, when compelled to put in an appearance, would not allow herself even to be touched by the visitor.

I never again doubted her judgment of anyone, and eventually I came to trust her judgment of other dogs, as well.

Gerda and I had gone to dinner with Trixie on the patio of a Balboa Island restaurant on at least fifty occasions, sometimes just the three of us, often with friends. She had always been the perfect child, causing no disturbance of any kind.

Then on a warm August night, when every table on the patio was occupied with customers, our girl glimpsed a dog on the farther side of the street, half a block away, with its master. Her hackles rose. She sprang to her feet and barked ferociously three times.

She was an exceptionally feminine girl and as gentle as a bunny rabbit, but her voice sounded as big and fierce as that of a 120-pound German shepherd on steroids. Her first bark caused the diners at the other tables to jump half out of their chairs.

I snared her collar, pulled her head close to me, and clamped her mouth shut with my right hand. Employing the command to stop barking, which I had never used before, I said, "Quiet."

She growled through this makeshift muzzle, but settled when I repeated, "Quiet." She tried to press her tongue between her teeth to lick my fingers. Knowing that she would be silent now, I let go of her.

To the other diners, who were all looking at us as if wondering which among them would be the first to be eaten, I said, "I'm sorry for the disturbance. We've brought her here dozens of times, and she never before barked."

A man at one of the farther tables said, "No problem. She's a good dog, and she knows a bad one when she sees it. That beast she barked at is extremely dangerous. It's attacked smaller dogs, and everyone who lives on the island is afraid of it for good reason."

Trixie had tried to warn me that X was deranged. Now she warned *off* the neighborhood canine bully.

We ordered her a plain, broiled chicken breast.

Trixie not only had a nose for trouble, but she never hesitated to stand up to trouble, as well.

•

When we lived in Harbor Ridge, each morning we followed the same route for Trixie's morning walk: out of our cul-de-sac and then south along Ridgeline, the cleverly named street that followed the top of the ridge. If we went north on Ridgeline, we came at once to a long steep hill that didn't offer Trixie the kind of terrain on which she preferred to toilet. Since potty was the first priority of the walk, south was the sole viable choice.

A block and a half from our house, on Ridgeline, a new family moved in with the biggest rottweiler we had ever seen. In the early morning, this brute—call him Big Dog—lay on a balcony that, because of some peculiar architecture, hung only seven feet off the ground. As we approached on the public sidewalk, which lay perhaps twenty feet from the balcony, Big Dog acted as if he had seen *Jurassic Park* and was a velociraptor wannabe. Saliva foaming from his mouth, he barked and snarled. He threw himself repeatedly against the balcony railing, which shook with every impact as if it would splinter into a million I-Ching sticks.

Because Trixie had once been bitten by a bad dog, Gerda and I—and Linda on the weekday afternoon walks—carried pepper spray to defend against another attack. This repellent discourages any dog in mid-charge but does no permanent damage. Passing Big Dog, we kept the pepper spray ready, an index finger resting on the discharge button. The rottweiler had not been tethered to anything. He was so big that he could have gotten over the balcony railing with ease and dropped seven feet to the lawn without injury. He didn't seem to realize with what little effort he could break free.

Morning after morning, Trixie led us past Big Dog without giving him a single glance. She kept her head high and did not hurry to get beyond his domain. In fact, she adopted a more leisurely pace during that half block. For two months, she showed no concern, though Gerda and I were grinding our teeth until we were a block beyond Big Dog.

One day, in July, Trixie had enough. Gerda was walking her that morning, and Big Dog flew into a great frenzy, throwing himself at the railing with reckless abandon, barking and snarling as if he would chew his way through the wooden pales. Abruptly, Ms. Trixie turned toward the enormous creature for the first time, and she started across the lawn toward the balcony.

Alarmed, Gerda tried to pull her back, but Trixie was too strong—and too determined—to be restrained. As far as Trix was concerned, this was Waterloo, and the bully was going down as surely as Napoleon did. Approaching the balcony, she began to bark, using every decibel of her surprisingly loud voice. At first, Big Dog answered her, but when he tried to shout her into silence, she cranked up the volume to match his.

By the time Trixie halted directly below Big Dog, barking up at him, Gerda wondered if, following the inevitable attack, she would be able to leave the hospital by Christmas. Trix gave Big Dog a thorough what-for and . . . after a minute, he stopped throwing himself at the railing. He grew still and quiet, and then he decided he ought to lie down and relax. When she was quite sure she had made her point with the rottweiler, Trixie fell silent, led Gerda to the sidewalk once more, and continued their morning walk.

Big Dog never again barked at us. Every morning, he remained lying on the balcony floor, watching as Trixie strolled past with either Gerda or me. Trix had never been worried about him because she had known that he was all bluster and no bite. Having read his character clearly, she put him in his place only when he became too annoying for her to continue to ignore him.

With her refined nose, Trixie could identify which humans and dogs were trouble—and which were not.

WHEN TRIXIE SPOKE, we learned to listen.

She sometimes went months without issuing a single sound louder than a sigh or a curious little grumble of discontent, which didn't even qualify as a growl. You might think, therefore, that on those rare occasions when she barked, we would at once be concerned and would want to know what motivated her to speak.

Instead, we became so accustomed to her silence, we reacted to a bark as if it were aberrant behavior that we must gently discourage lest we set her on a slippery slope from quiet companion to barking basket case. Cut us some slack: We are, after all, just human beings.

One Saturday, Gerda and I were working in our adjacent

offices, she on bookkeeping, I on a novel with an approaching deadline. As quitting hour drew near, we agreed on pizza for dinner. Thin-crust DiGiorno pizza has been such a significant part of our lives that we may at any moment pass some biological tipping point and begin to exude the aromas of cheese and pepperoni from our pores. Gerda went to the kitchen to preheat the oven, then returned to her office to finish her data entries.

About fifteen minutes later, having approached my desk without making a sound, Trixie let out a single tremendous bark. I shot from my chair as if it were a cannon and I were a clown.

Gravity brought me down again. Because I feared losing the tone of a paragraph that I hoped to finish before dinner, I responded to Trixie with the command I had used only once before, "Quiet."

She padded away. From Gerda's office came a window-rattling bark. I heard Gerda say, "Quiet, Miss Trixie. You scared me."

Returning to my work space with sneak-thief stealth, the golden one launched me from my chair again with two furious barks. She gave me a look of extreme disapproval. Her raised ears, flared nostrils, and body language indicated she had important and urgent news to convey.

Feeling as if I were Lassie's dad, trying to determine if this time Timmy had fallen down an abandoned well or was trapped inside a burning barn, I said, "What is it, girl? Show me what's wrong."

She hurried out of the room, and I followed her.

•

Our offices are in a separate wing of the house, isolated from the main living areas. Trixie trotted along the hallway where I shelve one copy each of about five thousand editions of my books in various languages. On a tough writing day, this collection encourages me: Having finished novels before, I will surely finish the current one.

The office hall connected to the main hall, where Trixie turned right. She picked up her pace, glancing back to see if I had wandered to a window to admire the red New Zealand impatiens in the courtyard. The short attention span of people can frustrate a dog on a mission.

I pursued her out of the hall. Halfway across the living room, I detected the faint acrid scent of something burning. Running now, Trixie barked one more time, to be sure that I would not stop at a sofa to rearrange the throw pillows.

In the kitchen, tentacles of thin gray smoke slithered out of the vent holes below an oven door. Each Thermador had a fan that sucked odors and fumes up a dedicated flue, dispersing them above the roof. The sooty octopoidal arms writhing into the room must mean the ventilation fan was overwhelmed by the volume of smoke inside the oven.

Not good.

Peering through the view window, I saw an object afire. For a moment, I couldn't identify the thing through the obscuring smoke, and then I saw that it was a burning hand, standing on the stump of its wrist.

A burning hand!

Those who have never read my novels often think, incorrectly, that I write horror stories. If you are one of those, you might expect that we discover burning body parts in our oven with some regularity. I assure you we do not.

This was a new experience for me and so macabre that for an instant I half expected the burning hand to wave or to give me the okay sign, or to make a rude gesture—but then I realized that it was not a hand after all. An oven mitt had been left in the Thermador the previous evening.

I switched off the oven and watched through the window in the door as the flames subsided, having consumed the oxygen available to them. Gradually the ventilation fan drew the last of the smoke up the flue, and the air in the kitchen began to clear as well.

The charred mitt looked more threatening than when it had been ablaze. I decided that it *wanted* me to open the oven door, so I left the cleanup to someone else.

From a distance too great for the human nose to detect even the faintest scent of fire, Trixie smelled disaster pending. That night we gave her extra treats—but only on the condition that she would never mention this incident to Smokey the Bear.

XIV

freedom of speech

IF A DOG gains a few pounds, it is not in the least concerned, because it lacks human vanity. Besides, a dog enjoys the perfect disguise for physical flaws: fur.

Were fur transplants to become available for human beings, I would be first in line, seeking a head-to-toe makeover, after which I would personally ensure the profitability of bakeries and ice cream shops throughout southern California.

A few pounds over our desired weight and determined to diet, Gerda and I made a pact to eat light meals for a week. At dinner on a restaurant patio with Trixie, we had salads without dressing and grilled chicken breasts with squash and carrots on the side. When we finished, we felt virtuous—but hungry. We didn't want to abandon all discipline and stuff ourselves with dessert, but the thought of a second salad held no more appeal than eating our table napkins. In a pinch, I can with alarming swiftness reason myself into doing the unreasonable, and though I usually can't get Gerda to abandon her characteristic prudence, she's more vulnerable when she's hungry. I made a case for finishing this diet dinner with an order of nachos, which I argued were suitable for anorexics if you just said, "Hold the sour cream." Guacamole, cheese, corn chips, and black beans were what reed-thin supermodels survived on for years at a time, or so I had read in Wikipedia or somewhere equally reliable. Gerda was in a mood to be conned, and the nachos were brought to the table on a platter large enough to hold a roast pig.

We are generally so disciplined that we never before ordered nachos in the years Trixie had been with us. The symphony of aromas stirred previously unknown passions in her, and she rose from the patio to sit beside my chair, a look of desperate longing on her face.

I was a bad boy, offering her three or four corn chips with melted cheese and a touch of guacamole. "Want some nachos, Short Stuff?" I didn't have to force them on her. She took them one by one, crunching them with great pleasure, but when I said, *"No más,"* she settled to the flagstones once more.

Once motivated people with strong willpower set themselves upon a sensible dietary regimen, they cannot easily be tempted to stray to the culinary dark side. The following night, Gerda and I had salads with chopped chicken and concluded dinner with another platter of nachos.

Again, I favored Trixie with a few cheese-slathered corn chips moistened with guacamole. "Want some nachos?" As before, she did not turn up her nose at them. She recognized a heart-friendly dish when she saw one. Heart-friendly and heart-healthy are different things, but it seems to me that anything that lifts the heart can't be bad for it, though I acknowledge that I'm no cardiologist.

We broke the spiral of madness and didn't have nachos again during the following three months. We lost the few pounds that we had set out to lose, without resorting either to liposuction or to amputation.

Fully twelve weeks after the two nacho binges, I was in Linda's office, where Trixie was lying happily on her bed with her forelimbs draped over a giant plush-toy lobster. Linda, Elaine, and I got into a conversation about new restaurants. I had come all the way across the house to their office to see if they were actually working at their desks or whether their chairs were occupied by mannequins cleverly disguised to look like them. I also came for a contract file that I needed to review. I would, of course, eventually leave their office without the contract file, return to my office, and have to come all the way back through the house again, which would amuse them more than caring employees ought to be amused. In the meantime, as restaurant recommendations were flying, Linda said, "And, oh, if you go there, you *have* to order their fabulous nachos."

The instant that the magic word was spoken, Trixie exploded off her bed, knocking aside the plush-toy lobster, and raced to Linda to gaze at her adoringly, waiting for cheese-slathered corn chips with a trace of guacamole, tail keeping time suitable to the latter bars of "Bolero," drool dripping from her jowls. Perhaps she'd heard the word four times each night at the restaurant, eight times altogether, yet after three months, Trixie responded instantly upon hearing it once more.

After five years of French classes in high school and college, I can no longer speak a coherent sentence in that language. This seems to me to suggest that either French would be more profitably studied if one were rewarded daily with nachos for learning—or that with the proper incentives, dogs can learn French.

In either case, Trixie's response to that delectable word puts the lie to some theories of dog intelligence and dog memory. It also suggests that dogs have a better grasp on the meaning of life than do a significant number of us.

No, a plate of nachos is not the meaning of life. But finding joy in things as humble as a plate of nachos is an important step toward the discovery of meaning.

•

Too many of us die without knowing transcendent joy, in part because we pursue one form or another of materialism. We seek meaning in possessions, in pursuit of cosmic justice for earthly grievances, in the acquisition of power over others. But one day Death reveals that life is wasted in these cold passions, because zealotry of any kind precludes love except of the thing that is idolized.

On the other hand, dogs eat with gusto, play with exuberance, work happily when given the opportunity, surrender themselves to the wonder and the mystery of their world, and love extravagantly. Envy infects the human heart; if we envy, next we covet, and what we covet becomes the object of our all-consuming avarice. If we live without envy, with the humility and the joyful gratitude of dogs—nachos! ball! cuddle time!—we will be ready even for Death when he comes for us, content that we have made good use of the gift of life.

WHEN WE LIVED in Harbor Ridge, our daily walks took us past a complex of three community tennis courts carved into a hillside and approached by descending stairs shaded by tall trees. In the morning, shortly past dawn, and sometimes in the afternoon, no players were present. Trixie always wanted to explore the deserted courts and the surrounding landscape for discarded tennis balls.

On some occasions, no balls were found. During other searches, she discovered so many that our jacket pockets were bulging with them. After a successful hunt, she had more bounce in her step for the remainder of the walk. She sniffed at our stuffed pockets with delight akin to what Donald Duck's uncle Scrooge exhibited when gauging the depth of the fortune in his treasure bin.

One day, Gerda returned home from the morning walk with a single tennis ball that she presented to me as if it were an object of great mystery and solemn meaning. There had been a moment during the search of the courts that had sent a pleasant shiver of wonder through her, followed by a feeling too sweet to be called sadness but too tender to be called anything else. She hesitated to explain, as though what she had to tell me would sound outlandish.

Gerda never invents or exaggerates. Indeed, sometimes she strips away the colorful details of a story because, though true, they seem to her to detract from the primary facts. If indeed her story sounded outlandish, the real event must have been twice as incredible.

As always, Trixie had wanted to hunt tennis balls. She led Gerda down the steps from court to court, also searching the shrubs and drainage swales for prizes that aggressive players had slammed over the fences. She found only disappointment.

Gerda ascended to the street, and Trix accompanied her. As they reached the sidewalk, our girl halted and looked back at the courts. Gerda said, "Let's go," but Trixie didn't obey. She resisted her leash. Looking up at her mom, she opened her mouth and thrust her muzzle forward as though straining to produce a sound—then spoke. "Baw."

This sound—pronounced like the word *awe* with a *b* in

front, slightly attenuated—was so unlike anything that came from Trixie before, was delivered with such an earnest expression, and was accompanied by such tension in our girl's entire body that Gerda hesitated to tug on the leash. Insisting upon eye contact, Trix repeated the word, "Baw." On hearing it a second time, Gerda realized that it sounded about as much like *ball* as a dog's vocal apparatus could allow.

After Trixie spoke a third time—"Baw"—Gerda asked, "Ball? Are you saying 'ball,' sweetie?"

Straining even harder than before, Short Stuff said, "Baw."

Gerda was aware of a tremendous yearning in the dog, a longing not for a ball but for the ability to convey the desire for a ball, and a fervent wish to convey it not with tail speak or body language or any of the communication techniques of her kind, but with a *word.*

Overcome by an extraordinary sense of intimacy between herself and her golden daughter, Gerda said, "We already looked for balls, sweetie. There aren't any this morning."

"Baw," Trixie repeated, almost beseechingly.

Relenting, Gerda said, "All right, let's look again."

The instant the leash went slack, Trixie led Gerda to the stairs once more. They descended halfway, whereupon Trix departed the steps to thrust under a shrub. When she pulled back and raised her glorious head, she held a tennis ball in her mouth.

Not only content to have found this treasure but jubilant

about having conveyed her awareness of it with a word, Trixie continued the morning walk in an even more spirited fashion than usual, frequently glancing up at her mom and chewing emphatically on the ball.

Because for so long I had felt this dog yearning to be able to talk, I knew Gerda must be reporting exactly what occurred, though as was her tendency, she shaved the edges off the more colorful details in the interest of whittling the story to its essence.

The incident moved her. As tenderhearted as she had been toward our girl, she grew even more so after that morning.

A couple of months later, I walked Trixie on a morning when my schedule was too full to give her an entire hour. I edited our route to forty minutes. Among other things, I deleted the tennis courts from our itinerary.

As we passed the courts, however, Trix tried to lead me toward them.

I said, "Not today, no time today, sugarpie," and gently tugged the leash to keep her moving.

She halted and wouldn't proceed, and when I crouched to scratch her chest and rub behind her ears, which I sometimes did to cajole rather than to command her to follow the rules, she contorted her face as if yawning, but she made no sound. Then she thrust her head toward me, not seeking further affection, but to focus my attention as she said, "Baw."

Because I had not thought about Gerda's experience in weeks, Trixie's expressed desire surprised me. The word was spoken exactly as Gerda pronounced it, but when face-to-face with Trix, the meaning was far clearer than I would have thought. Perhaps that impressive clarity was because she sold the word with the tension in her body, with the expression on her face, with the outward curl of her upper lip that exaggerated the shape that the human mouth gives to the word *ball,* and with the intensity of her stare.

"Baw."

This was not the mimicry of a parrot, words repeated but with no meaningful context. This word and the shaping of it had been thought through, and she used it precisely when it could gain for her what she wanted.

"Baw."

In this remarkable moment, she tried to bridge the gulf between one who could not speak and one who could, and she succeeded in that she conveyed her meaning. This achievement was inspiriting but also sobering and even slightly sad, for it was a triumph that emphasized the impossibility of ever having another like it.

I kissed her brow and said, "You're right, Short Stuff. If I've got to edit your walk, I should never delete the part of it that you most enjoy. Let's go hunt some tennis balls."

She found enough of them that morning to fill all the pockets in my jacket.

XV

water, wonder, work

GOLDEN RETRIEVERS ARE water dogs, bred to swim into a lake and bring back the duck you shot. Because I loved Daffy and Donald since childhood, I never shot a duck, which would have felt like toonicide. Trixie had no opportunity to prove her merit as a hunter's dog.

Our house in Harbor Ridge had a pool, however, where we learned she was a better swimmer than her mom or dad. Prior to adopting Trix, we had seldom used the pool, but when she stood at the French doors, staring at the sun-glistered water and sighing, we couldn't resist taking the plunge with her. Gerda, who never had the opportunity to learn to swim, decided to teach herself with the assistance of a strap-on flotation device. As Gerda paddled earnestly from one end of the pool to the other, Trix swam with her, but not at her side; instead, our golden girl continually—literally—swam circles around her mom all the way from one end of the pool to the other, as if to show how it should be done, or as if making another joke.

Although she loved to swim, Trixie wouldn't enter the pool until invited. Sometimes she used the steps, but usually she gathered her legs together, tensed, and launched off the coping, making a huge splash. During an hour of play, she returned to the deck ten times, rested for a few minutes, then barreled into the water again.

We have pliable-foam pool floats coated in rubber, on which we can stretch out to tan. The second time I took Trixie to play in the water, I drew one of these floats into the pool when she climbed out to take a rest. Aboard it, lying on my back, I glanced at her. She watched me with great interest, head raised and thrust forward, intrigued to see me drifting languidly on the water without effort.

I basked in the sun until overcome by a feeling that I was about to find myself in a Daffy Duck cartoon. When I opened my eyes, Trixie stood at the edge of the pool, legs bunched under her, grinning maniacally. "No!" I cried, but she jumped, slamming onto the float, turning it upside-down and dumping both of us into the drink.

Surfacing, I saw her pawing frantically at the float, trying to clamber onto it, while it bobbled and turned in the water. I held it steady, forcing one side under water so her forelimbs could easily slide onto it, and then, by holding the float with one hand and giving her butt a boost with the other, I got her aboard.

Judging by her expression, this was one of the most amazing and delightful experiences of her life. She lay with her back legs splayed, her forelimbs bent at the elbows and straight in front of her, head raised, looking around in wonder. *Floating! On water! Without paddling! Genius! My dad's a genius!*

When I towed her from one end of the pool to the other and then back again, she panted with excitement. And she made the most winsome sound, not a whine or whimper, but a thin sweet expression of total doggy ecstasy. *I'm moving! Through water! Without swimming! Brilliant! My dad's brilliant!*

At first shakily, then with confidence, she stood on the float while I pulled it the length of the pool again. Surfer girl.

Over the years, she spent more time being towed around than she did swimming. She taught herself to get aboard without help, by pushing the float into a corner of the pool and wedging it there, where it couldn't bobble away from her while she climbed onto it.

I marveled at the chain of reasoning necessary for her to reach the conclusion that she could take control of this situation.

While lying on the float, Trix liked to play a game with me involving a thin, hollow rubber ball with an air hole in it. I held the ball between thumb and forefinger, moving it back and forth on the surface of the water while she watched intently. Suddenly, I pulled the ball under without squeezing the air out of it. Excited, she thrust one paw into the water, trying to grasp the treasure as I moved it left, right, and in circles. Then I brought it in front of her face again, still under water. Because the air remained in the ball, and because the air hole was toward the bottom of the pool, the ball soared to the surface when released, rising with enough energy to erupt a few inches into the air. Trixie watched it rising, trying to gauge the ascent, and often snatched it from the air, with her teeth, as it popped out of the pool.

One day, as I towed her around on her raft, she took the ball between her paws and pushed it under the water as she had seen me do. As we moved along, she stared contemplatively at the submerged blue sphere. When I paused and the raft grew still, she released the ball, which popped out of the water. With her mouth, she caught it in midair. She repeated this a few times, intent on the process, and then raised her head and met my eyes.

I held her stare for a moment and then whispered, "You are one smart little girl."

She grinned and panted, pleased by the praise.

Short Stuff was learning new tricks, and—like us—even a new perspective. During her first few years as a Koontz, Trixie seemed focused exclusively on things at ground level. She was uninterested in birds, as if oblivious of any realm above a rooftop. I hadn't thought how strange this was until I considered that in its historic role as a partner in the hunt, a retriever must track the flight and fall of the shot fowl if it is to find the bird and return it to its master's game bag. Perhaps Trix's education as an assistance dog trained her out of her appreciation for the sky.

When encountering rabbits grazing on a lawn, she greatly enjoyed stalking them, though she never chased and would not actually seize one. She always approached the target bunny with exaggerated stealth: slowly raise one paw at a time, freeze on three legs, wait, wait, leisurely reach forward, place the paw on the ground again, wait, wait, and now the next paw. . . . She crept up on the prey in a slow-motion doggy ballet, and even when the rabbit saw her from the first, she often got quite near before it bolted. If she didn't close much of the gap, she continued on her walk without comment, but when she got near enough to have taken her prey if she had wanted it, she looked up at me and grinned as if to say, *See, Dad, I love the ways of people, but I still know the way of the wild.*

Trix and I were swimming—well, she was lying on her float while I pulled her back and forth in the lap pool—when the Goodyear blimp, a fixture in southern California skies, appeared at low altitude along the coast. It turned inland toward the ridge on which we lived.

Cruising at a height of perhaps two hundred feet, the blimp was an impressive sight. Its engine and propellers made less noise than the swimming-pool pump, therefore the vessel loomed as silently as an apparition.

Because of the blimp's low altitude, Trixie spotted it during its approach, and she expressed her astonishment by letting the ball fall out of her mouth. She watched in wonder. When the vessel passed directly overhead, seeming so low that I could throw the ball and hit it, Trixie's gaze remained riveted on it. From the back of her throat issued that sweet, high-pitched sound of delight, and her wet tail thumped on the float. She tracked the blimp for several minutes, until it was a dot in the distance.

After that summer day, though she still stalked rabbits until she spooked them away, she remained aware of the sky as she had not been previously. She became interested in birds and passing aircraft. Like a door, the world above had opened to her.

By Trixie's striking intelligence, by her sense of humor, by the uncanny moments when she seemed to reveal a spiritual dimension, she renewed my sense of the mystery of life. Now it seemed that the looming blimp restored to her a small lost measure of her own wonder.

And at our beach house one morning, a similar incident deepened Trixie's appreciation of the harbor.

The pavilion on our pier, which overlooked the gangway and the boat slip, was spacious enough to accommodate a sofa and dining table with four chairs. This was the perfect place from which to watch the Christmas boat parade or to have a glass of wine before bed, when the lights on the farther shore shimmered across the dark water.

During one of our infrequent visits, Gerda and I were having breakfast at the pavilion table and reading the Sunday newspapers, when I heard a soft burst of sound, the *whoosh* of escaping air. I assumed it was a noise related to one of the many boats docked and moored nearby, a venting of the bilge or something too nautical and arcane for me to understand.

The third time the sound came, it was followed by Trixie's winsome little squeal of delight. She was behind me, lying on the deck, her forepaws hanging over the edge, head pushed under the lower horizontal of the railing, staring down at something in the water.

Gerda and I knelt, flanking our girl, and saw a sea lion a few feet away, a creature weighing at least eight hundred pounds. It turned slowly in the water as if pirouetting for our entertainment. Because the tide was high, the surface of the harbor lay only two or three feet below the floor of the pier. The glistening black eyes of the sea lion seemed to remain focused on Trixie as slowly it turned, turned, turned.

Tremors passed through Short Stuff's body, and we gentled her with our hands, though she seemed to be less frightened than excited. When the sea lion concluded its performance and glided on its back under the pavilion, Trixie shot to her feet.

Abruptly I knew she would dive in after the creature when it reappeared.

Even as Trixie turned from us, I shouted, "Grab her collar!"

I missed getting hold of her, Gerda missed, Trixie scurried to the farther side of the structure, we scrambled after her, and we both gripped her collar an instant before she would have gone under the railing and into the drink.

Sea lions can be aggressive. I suppose the creature would have dived deep and away if Trixie plunged into the harbor beside it, but the possibility that she would have been harmed or even killed was not insignificant.

Now that she knew an exotic hidden world lay below the surface of the sea, Trixie wanted to explore it. Henceforth, every time we were on the pier, she watched the water for a school of fish, a raft of seaweed, anything mysterious, and then wanted at once to race down to the boat slip to have a closer look.

We had to keep her on a leash the last few times we went to the beach house. But every time she saw something in the water that she wanted to investigate, I hurried with her down the gangway, and we walked the boat slip together. Some days, we made this trip six or seven times an hour.

She was made especially nuts by the brown pelicans that dove for fish and surfaced, flying, far from the point at which they disappeared into the water. If they could live in both realms, in the air and below the surface of the sea, why couldn't both worlds be accessible to a water retriever with webs between her toes?

•

For a dog, the world is an ever-expanding carnival of mysteries. Every new experience enchants, and every morning is full of promise.

As children, we share that attitude, but we evict it when we become adults, as if the knowledge that comes with experience needs to occupy that particular chamber of the mind, as if wonder must make way for wisdom. But wisdom without wonder is not true wisdom at all, but only a set of practical skills married to tactical shrewdness of one degree or another.

Wonder inspires curiosity, and curiosity keeps the mind from becoming sick with irrational ideologies and stultified with dogma.

WHEN I SAY that Trixie restored my sense of wonder, you might be curious to know what had happened to it. Life had happened to it.

My mother, a good person with a kind heart, had died after much suffering at the age of fifty-three. My father, a selfish and violent man who never met a vice he didn't like, lived to be eighty-three. Your sense of wonder relies in part on your perception that this world is founded on a system of natural law that is not only binding on humanity but that is expressed at least as often as not in the story of every life, in the choices people make and in the consequences thereof, a natural law that is like an awesome machine turning the gears of the world, a machine that is hidden under the surfaces of all things but is thrillingly revealed in occasional transcendent moments. My mother lived with faith and right reason, yearning for order, but reaped only disorder and an early death. My father, an apostle of disorder, had a long life full of the pleasures of the flesh that he prized, using and deceiving and betraying and defrauding people as a matter of routine, yet always escaping the punishment of the courts and the cosmos. The beautiful machine of natural law, of which I hoped to have a glimpse, remained hidden from me for a long time.

In my first job after college, working in that federal antipoverty initiative, I had expected to live my ideals. In mere months, I discovered that such programs didn't work, that in fact they were enormously destructive, that they were designed by a political class less interested in solving society's ills than in power and in using that power to enrich themselves and their cronies, whose appetites were as insatiable as those of hogs at a trough. Cynicism can corrode your sense of wonder.

At Mechanicsburg High School, I enjoyed teaching and had a knack for it, but the educational bureaucracy and the theories on which it fed proved to be the opposite of that beautiful machine of natural law, was instead a big, ever-growing, mindless, mechanical leviathan wreaking havoc as it ground through the decades, certain to produce eventually a generation of perfect barbarians. Seeing through to the truth under the illusions that have shaped you is important, but it can be dispiriting and can tie knots in your wonder.

Becoming a published and eventually a full-time writer was exciting and gratifying. But achieving success required a long, hard slog, during which the romance and the glamour and the nobility of the literary life proved to be more illusions waiting to be seen through. I had good literary agents and bad. The bad were horrendous, and the good ones never had a vision of my career that matched mine. My heroes had long been novelists, and although I met some writers who became good and cherished friends, Gerda and I found this community as a whole to be solipsistic and narcissistic and irrational to such a degree that when I showed her a newspaper story about a university study headlined 80 PERCENT OF PEOPLE WITH WRITING TALENT SHOW SIGNS OF SCHIZOPHRENIA, she said, "Can you believe it's only eighty percent?"

Even so, I remained happy and optimistic and industrious because three things kept my spirits high: Gerda and the love we shared; a deepening appreciation of the English language bound inextricably with a profound pleasure in storytelling; close friends, which included some people with whom I worked, such as my editor Tracy Devine.

While restoring my diminished sense of wonder to the fullness and brightness that characterized it in childhood, Trixie inspired me also to share with readers my recovered delight in the mystery of life. At a time in most writing careers when the work has become cast in a mold that cannot be broken, when enthusiasm for new techniques has given way to a preference for the comfort of the familiar, when characters are old friends with new names and different wardrobes from those they wore before, when stories follow patterns long established, I felt a tide of creativity breaking me loose from the encrusting barnacles of thirty years of storytelling. I began writing novels unlike any I had done before, taking risks with narratives, themes, and characters that I would not have taken previously, that I would not have recognized *could* be taken. The greater challenge of these new books brought me enormous pleasure that at times approached a sustained rapture. The difficulty encouraged in me a devotion to the task that not only sharpened the fiction but also clarified my views on life, focused me on first things, returned me to a faith from which I had drifted, and not only returned me but also secured me there forever by virtue of a rigorous intellectual argument with myself that resulted in a new understanding of the wisdom of faith and the truth of life's abiding mystery.

Some dog, huh?

Previously, in addition to books of more modest word counts, I had written two massive novels—*Strangers* and *Dark Rivers of the Heart*—which were well received, but in which it seems to me the struggle of the writer is sometimes glimpsed on the page. The first book I wrote while Trixie was with us, *False Memory,* turned out to be the longest book I had written to date, but tighter than the two aforementioned works. The novel is an allegory, and though in the past I had introduced humor in a suspenseful story, I approached *False Memory* as a comic novel and a suspense novel in equal measure. The story concerns the problem of Evil. It recognizes the truth that evil acts are out of sync with the ordered nature of the world, and therefore are irrational, absurd. The absurdity of Evil and of those who serve it is the source of our greatest defense against darkness: laughter. The antagonist of *False Memory* is as unconsciously amusing as he is terrifying, and often during the writing of his scenes, I laughed out loud at his pretensions and his self-delusion.

The new direction my work took with that book and all I have written since derived from four revelations:

First, I arrived at the certainty that Trixie possessed a soul as real as mine. Intelligence signifies more than an ability to relate cause to effect and to solve problems, both of which she could do. The fact that the universe exists is the most astonishing thing of all, but the second greatest astonishment is the existence of creatures, whether human beings or dogs or others, that can reason and learn, that are not driven solely by instinct. Consciously and unconsciously, the intelligent being searches for meaning and seeks its purpose. This effort cannot be pointless, because Nature inspires it in us, and Nature is never wasteful. The universe is efficient: Matter becomes energy; energy becomes matter; one form of energy is converted into another; the balance is always changing, but the universe is a closed system from which no particle of matter or wave of energy is ever lost. Nature does not waste, and if intelligent beings by their very nature seek meaning, then there must be meaning to be found. By Trixie's intelligence, by her sense of wonder, she revealed a seeking soul—and led me to a reconsideration not only of the mystery of life but of the mystery of my own soul and destiny.

My second revelation was the recognition of the unblemished innocence of her soul compared to mine or to that of any human being. She didn't need a new Ferrari or a week in Vegas to know joy. For her, bliss was a belly rub, a walk on a sunny day—or in the rain, for that matter—an extra cookie when it wasn't expected, a cuddle, a kind word. She lived to love and to receive love, which is the condition of angels.

Third, I understood that the joy arising from innocence, from harmony with nature and natural law, must be the most exhilarating feeling either dog or human could hope to experience. Dogs' joy is directly related to the fact that they do not deceive, do not betray, and do not covet. Innocence is neither naive nor unhip; innocence is the condition of deepest bliss.

Fourth, I came to realize that the flight from innocence so characteristic of our time is a leap into absurdity and insanity.

If Gerda and I had decided to delay accepting a dog from CCI and later received another golden, instead of Trixie, or if we'd decided not ever to have a dog, I wonder who I would be, these eleven years later. Whatever Dean Koontz I would be, I would not be the Dean Koontz I am now. Considering the potentially momentous nature of even the smallest decisions we make, we ought to be terrified and humbled, we ought to be filled with gratitude for every grace we receive.

XVI

time and memory

EACH TIME I write about dogs in a novel or a work of nonfiction, I receive a few letters accusing me of anthropomorphizing them, of ascribing human attributes to mere animals.

Some of my correspondents have an aversion to dogs, and they are annoyed to see one portrayed with what they deem is excess affection.

Others write from a moral high ground, which they claim in the name of their religion. They are certain to a fault that God's grace extends only to human beings, that other living things on this Earth are pretty much like the low-paid extras that fill out crowd scenes in movies. I suppose they must interpret the biblical admonition that God knows of every sparrow's death to mean not that He cares for all of His creatures in this fallen world, but instead that He has a worldwide surveillance system so awesome that even Homeland Security could not replicate it.

A few correspondents reject the concept of human exceptionalism and believe that any animal is *superior* to any person. If I ascribe human qualities and characteristics to a dog, these folks feel that I am demeaning canines.

Finally, an animal psychologist or a zoologist, or a naturalist of another kind, will assure me that the human qualities and emotions I see in dogs are not what they appear to be, that the mind of any animal is radically different from ours. Depending on their area of expertise, they will assert all manner of astonishing things: that a dog has no sense of its individuality, no true self-awareness, as we do; that a dog's mind is insufficiently complex to engender emotions; that a dog cannot reason from a cause to an effect.

Nonsense.

All of us, scientists and nonscientists alike, find it difficult almost to the point of impossibility to see the world through another human being's mind, which is why we're continually surprised by what even our friends and neighbors are capable of doing. The serial killer next door is routinely described as a quiet, nice, ordinary guy by those who imagined that they knew him.

What a leap it then is to insist that we can know absolutely how the mind of *another species* works. The great advantages of a mutual language and a shared culture fail us daily in our efforts to understand our own kind. With dogs, the experts have only theory. Evidently, the prospect that the world at its deepest level rests on a mystery we cannot solve this side of death is so terrifying to some that our wondrous dogs must be regarded as nothing more than meat machines lest their true and astonishing nature should cause us to consider how magical is our very existence

One caveat: When discussing the possible thoughts, reasoning, and intentions of a dog, we must remember that overall intelligence varies from breed to breed. Levels of intelligence also vary from individual to individual within the same breed, just as it varies from one human being to another. Trixie was a very smart golden.

I HAVE OFTEN read and been told that dogs have no sense of time. I don't believe this, but what I do believe is that the people who say it have no sense, period.

Believing dogs have no sense of the passage of time, you should not be concerned if you leave old Spot alone for one hour or four hours when you go out for an evening. In either case, his perception supposedly will be that you have been gone awhile, for a period he can't measure, perhaps for a minute or perhaps for a day.

Trixie possessed such a precise and reliable sense of time that we would not have needed clocks or watches to keep her on her daily schedule. After a breakfast of kibble, she received an apple-cinnamon rice cake at eleven thirty, just before her midday walk, and then a dish of kibble at three-thirty, prior to her afternoon walk. Gerda, Linda, Elaine, and I daily experienced Trixie's uncanny promptitude. Never later than the appointed time, but never more than a minute or two earlier, she came to whoever had custody of her; with the tap of a raised paw or with a bump of her nose, or by placing her head in your lap and rolling her eyes, she announced that in case you hadn't noticed, the hour had come for food, exercise, and toileting. Year after year, she announced these daily routines with accuracy.

Eventually, we grew so accustomed to the reliability of the clock in Trixie's head that it ceased to amaze us, but we never stopped being impressed by the way she adapted to daylight-saving time. When we sprang forward an hour in the spring and then fell back an hour in the autumn, she was never an hour late or early, but still to the minute in sync with the reset clocks.

When she came to us, Trixie accepted the work schedule that Gerda and I maintained, which kept us at our desks until at least six o'clock, often until seven or later, though we were up every morning by five thirty or six.

Within two weeks, however, Trixie decided that we were insane for working past five o'clock, and she set out upon a campaign to free us from our offices at a normal quitting hour. One day, promptly at five, she came to the farther side of my U-shaped desk and issued not a bark, but a soft woof. When I turned away from the computer to discover what disturbed her, I could see only her glorious big head above the desk. She stared at me with an intense expression that Gerda called the "Ross look." Ross Cerra, her father, had a frown of disapproval that could wilt a fresh flower from a distance of forty feet. After telling Trix that it was not yet quitting time and that she must be patient, I turned my attention to the keyboard once more.

Fifteen minutes later, she issued another *sotto voce* woof. This time her head was poked around the corner of the desk. Her Ross look had grown so solemn that Ross himself could not have matched its effect. Again, I told her the time to quit had not arrived, and I returned to the scene that I was writing.

At five thirty, she came directly to my chair and sat staring at me. When I didn't acknowledge her, she inserted her head under the arm of my chair, squinching her ears and fur, peering up at me with such a forlorn expression that I couldn't ignore her. A few minutes later, I knocked off early and took her outside to play.

The following afternoon, when she woofed softly at five o'clock, I didn't yet understand that she was on a crusade to change our lives. As before, she started from the farther side of my desk, poked her head around the corner fifteen minutes later, and came to my chair at five thirty. When she squeezed her head under the chair arm and implored me with her melancholy gaze, I realized she had a strategy and the tactics to fulfill it.

I tried to defend the sanctity of my work schedule, but her wiles were irresistible. Within two weeks, we regularly knocked off work at five thirty, and within a month, because of the clock in Trixie's head and her diligent insistence, five o'clock became the official end of the workday in Koontzland.

SOME WILL TELL you that dogs' memories are short, that they retain only what has been drilled into them through repetitive training and what relates directly to their basic needs of food, water, and shelter.

My polite response to that is, "Balderdash."

Vito and Lynn, who had been vacationing at our beach house when Trixie came to us from CCI, returned the following year to stay two weeks again. On their first evening there, we drove a Ford Explorer to the peninsula to pick them up for dinner, and Trixie rode in the cargo space, gazing out the tailgate window at the world receding.

When greeting people whom she had met before, Short Stuff's enthusiasm was directly proportional to how much fun they had been on the previous occasion. As usual, Vito and Lynn had been more fun each day than an entire amusement park, and that was *before* the cocktail hour. When they got into the backseat, Trixie lost her composure. She wiggled excitedly, tail slap-slap-slapping the walls of the cargo space. She made that winsome, hardly audible squeal of ecstasy in the back of her throat. Unable to contain herself, she sprang into the backseat, between them, which she had never done with anyone before, and lavished on them the Tongue of Love, though she rarely licked.

She had seen them several days on their previous visit, but not again for a year. Yet her behavior confirmed beyond doubt that she not only recognized them but also remembered that they had been great company. No other explanation holds water, especially since Vito had long ago stopped wearing that liver-scented cologne.

But Trixie displayed remarkable long-term memory, as well. In one instance, going back to her earliest days as a puppy . . .

A year earlier, when Vito and Lynn had accompanied us to the CCI campus in Oceanside, with the crew of *Pinnacle,* Gerda and I asked Judi Pierson what would be done with the large portion of their land not yet used. She said they hoped to build a residential facility in which each class of people with disabilities could stay for the two weeks that were required to learn how properly to handle and care for their dogs.

At that time, those who were chosen to be teamed with a dog (henceforth "team partners") had to stay in area motels and motor inns during the two-week "boot camp." This was unsatisfactory for at least three reasons. Some of the team partners could not easily afford those two weeks of lodging and dining out. Older motels could not usually accommodate people in wheelchairs, and some of the team partners could find rooms only miles from the campus, which made an exhausting day of instruction even more draining. And with the class scattered to numerous locations every night, there was less camaraderie, fewer opportunities for the team partners to cheer on one another.

CCI envisioned a wheelchair-accessible residential facility on the Oceanside campus, with rooms large enough to accommodate the team partners and their family members, with also a full-service catering kitchen, a dining room, a lounge, and other features. Gerda and I agreed to make a grant to CCI through our charitable foundation, for the purpose of constructing this residential facility.

A few years later, the grand opening celebration was tied to the graduation of the first class—numbering ten or twelve, I think—that had stayed in the new residence hall. When Gerda and I arrived with Trixie, we were surprised to see a monument sign on the front lawn that identified this as the DEAN AND GERDA KOONTZ CAMPUS of Canine Companions for Independence. We do not ask any charity to which we contribute to emblazon our names on anything. It had not occurred to us that this would be done as a surprise. While we prefer to keep a low profile, CCI is so close to our hearts that we were more touched than embarrassed by this tribute.

Every parking space along the street was taken, and neither Gerda nor I realized that a space in the CCI lot, near the front door, was reserved for us. We followed a road to the top of a long hill overlooking the campus and parked at a considerable distance.

When Trixie jumped down from the back of the SUV, she was adamant about getting to CCI *quickly*. This was the campus where she received her six months of advanced training and from which she had graduated with Jenna years ago. I assumed that she was excited by nothing more than nostalgia for the old days when she had been the class clown. No horse could have pulled harder than Trixie pulled me, and on the way down the hill, I thought she would drag me off my feet. Gerda kept saying, "Wait, wait, slow down," and as I struggled to keep my balance on the slope, I couldn't explain that Trixie had for the first time in my experience become a rowdy girl who ignored all the rules of leash training.

If Trix continued this behavior once inside CCI, I would need to explain how I had allowed their perfectly trained young lady to be transformed into a candidate for a dogs-gone-wild video. Some of the blame might credibly be placed on an exuberant yellow Lab who lived across the street and was a bad influence, even though no such Lab existed, but I didn't have enough time to work out plausible details to support a claim that she had eaten fermented kibble.

In the dry and sunny day, the drooping trees did not whisper in the motionless air, but at a higher altitude, a breeze chased clouds toward the faraway coast. In the perfect stillness, shadows of clouds undulated across the ground, and seemed to be spirits invading this tranquil reality from a more turbulent parallel universe. Trixie's radiant coat shone red blond in the fleeting forms of shade, blond red in the brighter light, her flags fluffy and white in either condition. Perhaps the strangeness of still air and rampant shadows contributed to my impression that our golden girl's beauty was more ethereal than ever—even though she strained mightily on the leash, as if determined to pull me to my knees.

When we arrived at CCI, I hoped Trix would stop pulling, but my hope wasn't fulfilled. She hadn't yet arrived where she wished to be.

A few hundred people were in full celebration, standing in the hallways and between buildings in the courtyards. There might have been a hundred dogs in attendance, not just those who had graduated this day with their team partners, but also younger dogs in their training capes, with their puppy raisers, and release dogs, like Trixie, who were companions to the volunteers who gave so much time to CCI and made it purr like a high-performance engine.

Straining at the leash, Trixie led Gerda and me through the crowd, not the least interested in the double score of dogs she passed or in the people who called her name and reached out to pet her. At last she stopped nose to nose with another lovely golden retriever, their tails lashing with delight. Clearly, this must have been her destination from the moment she exited the SUV.

As the two dogs communed, Gerda and I chatted with the woman who had the other golden. When I described how determined Trixie had been to get to this very spot, she said, "Do you know what dog this is? It's Tinsey, one of Trixie's litter mates."

Most experts will say that a few weeks after the pups in a litter are separated, they no longer recognize one another as brothers and sisters. Insufficient long-term memory.

Hah. Years later, Trixie caught the scent of her sibling from a couple of hundred yards and would not rest until they had been reunited. Considering all the other dogs present that day, this bit of evidence, though anecdotal, convinces me that dogs can remember not only what they learn from repetitive training or what knowledge directly assists their survival, but also what most matters to them otherwise, and they can remember it for a long, long time.

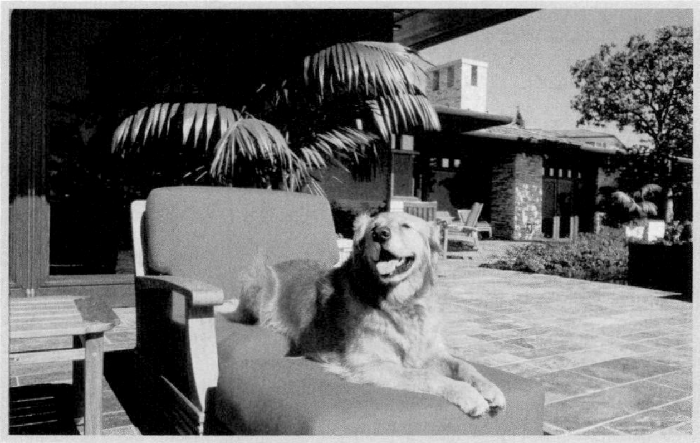

XVII

dogs and death

WHEN A BELOVED character in one of my novels dies, I must write about that death with the emotion and the reverence I would bring to a eulogy given for a real person. We all go into that dark, which is the darkness of God, the ultimate humbling of our prideful kind; therefore, death is a sacred subject requiring me to consider the native knowledge with which I was born, whether I am writing about the death of a fictional person, a real person, or a dog.

Current theory claims that dogs are unaware they will die. Theory does not deserve respect when it conflicts with our intuition and common sense, which are native to the mind and fundamental to sanity.

We might take comfort in this claim that dogs are unaware of their mortality because it lifts from dogs the fundamental fear with which we must live. But it's a false comfort, as anyone knows who has loved and been loved by a dog, and who has not surrendered his common sense.

Worse, in believing such a thing, we rob dogs of the profoundly moving stoicism that gives them immense dignity. When you have dogs, you witness their uncomplaining acceptance of suffering, their bright desire to make the most of life in spite of the limitations of age and disease, their calm awareness of the approaching end when their final hours come. They accept death with a grace that I hope I will one day be brave enough to muster.

We live in death, which is all around us, and waiting in us. Yet modern men and women—meaning not those people of this current age but those who embrace the modern prejudices—live as if death is not a part of life but only an end. They worship youth, live for the moment, in time and of time, with no capacity to imagine anything outside of time. They do not deny death as much as they repress the recognition of their intimate relationship with it. Death is given a place in their thoughts similar to that occupied by a childhood friend not seen in twenty years, known to be still out there in the old hometown, a thousand miles away, but not currently relevant.

A life-altering lesson can be learned by considering what dogs know about mortality and how they know it.

Intuition + common sense = dog wisdom.

Contention One: Dogs know. Dogs know they die.

Contention Two: By intuition, dogs know more about death than the mere fact of it.

A neighbor of ours heard commotion in the backyard and stepped outside to discover that a mountain lion had come out of the canyon and over the fence. The big cat, one of the most ferocious of all predators and seen seldom in these parts, was after the family dog.

Around the yard, across the patio, around the pool, the dog—let's call him Winslow—raced for his life, spun-jumped-scrambled from one hoped-for haven to another. Happily for both Winslow and his owner, the mountain lion allowed itself to be chased off with loud noise and a makeshift weapon. This is fortunate because the lion could have decided to go for a Big Mac instead of a small burger, and could have killed the owner as easily as it could have chowed down on Winslow, who was a third its size.

If dogs have no concept of their mortality, if they don't know they die, why did Winslow strive so frantically to avoid the mountain lion? Maybe the big cat only wanted to play. Maybe they could have had a great time with a tug toy.

We could say that *instinct* inspired Winslow to flee.

Instinct is an inborn pattern of activity or a tendency

to action, a natural impulse, genetically programmed. Bird migration in winter is one example, as is the pattern that the spider spins in its web.

Intuition is a higher form of knowledge than instinct. It is a direct perception of truth or fact, independent of any reasoning, knowledge neither derived from experience nor limited by it, such as that the whole is greater than a part, that two things each equal to a third thing are also equal to each other. Intuition also includes perceptions of space and spatial relationships, and an awareness of time.

Although instinct may exist in every creature from human beings to whales to field mice, it's also a quality of essentially brainless creatures like ants and goldfish, which have no intuition. Common sense tells us a dog is more like a human being than like an ant.

But even if it was just instinct that told Winslow to run from the mountain lion, did it tell him merely to run or specifically to run *because he would be eaten?*

You might say it doesn't matter which, because in either case, the action taken by Winslow was the same. But if Winslow knows he will be eaten, surely he knows he is mortal. Therefore, if one wishes to insist dogs are ignorant of their mortality, one must stick with the idea that it is enough for instinct to impel Winslow to run even if he does not know why he must escape the mountain lion.

But there will be many instances when Winslow or another of his kind will have seen a family dog or a house cat attacked and killed if not by the rare mountain lion, then by coyotes, which are more plentiful in these canyons.

So my next question is: Once Winslow has seen Fido or Fluffycat consumed by a coyote, does he finally realize what almost happened to him that day with the lion? Does he now recognize his own mortality?

To be consistent, if we support current theory, we must say no. If it was so easy for a dog to recognize he is mortal, all dogs would be wise to Death.

All right. After Winslow has seen Fido eaten, if he does not reason his way to the concept of mortality, what *does* he think has happened to the luckless dog? Does he think Fido now lives *inside* the coyote or that they have morphed together?

Perhaps some will reply that Winslow thinks nothing at all, that his brain is neither large enough nor wired in such a way as to allow him to ponder those questions. Fido was there. Fido is now not there. It means nothing to Winslow, who moves on with his day.

I don't believe anyone who has a much-loved dog can defend current theory past this point. Those who remain certain that Winslow never ponders Fido's fate may work with dogs in the laboratory but are invariably dogless in their private lives.

When a dog is your companion and not just your lab subject or your pet, when it is a member of the family and as lovingly observed as would be a child, you learn that the smarter breeds—and perhaps all breeds to different degrees—have greater intelligence than they are often said to have. Not only are they smart, they are also immensely *curious,* more curious than some of the people who speak with authority about them. And if their curiosity is encouraged, they can astonish with their ability to learn.

Thirty-five years ago, Bonnie Bergin realized that dogs were capable of serving as more than guiding eyes for the blind. She created the concept of the assistance dog for people with a wide range of disabilities, and she implemented that concept in Canine Companions for Independence. She later founded the Assistance Dog Institute, which became Bergin University for Canine Studies.

Not long ago she told me: "When I started down this road so many years ago, I would not have believed that one day I might say these dogs can be taught *anything*."

She has taught them to recognize the scent of grapevine-destroying pests so early in the infestation of a vineyard that the enterprise is saved, and only the first couple of infected vines need to be removed; large-scale pesticide spraying is not as necessary as it once was. She has taught them to smell cancer in a patient so early that the usual medical tests cannot yet detect the disease, and experiments in this area are ongoing.

"But it's true," Bonnie emphasized. "With patience and the right techniques, with reward training and respect for them, these dogs can be taught *anything*. The more they learn, the more they *can* learn."

Because for over twenty years I have seen canine intelligence in action at CCI and elsewhere, I have no patience for movies that sell the dog as a dumb, goofy, blundering agent of chaos. Nearly always, the problem is not the dog but the owners who cannot or do not bother to teach it as they would teach a child. A movie about dumb, goofy, blundering, agent-of-chaos humans and a wise long-suffering dog who loves them in spite of their idiocies is long overdue.

Dogs know.

Mike Martin, our friend and general contractor, who said he usually thought of anal glands when he thought of me, died suddenly of a massive heart attack before our new house was finished. He was only fifty-five years old.

We'd just gotten up that morning when Mike's wife, Edie, called and told Gerda that Mike had been rushed to the hospital, evidently having suffered a heart attack. He was such a big, strong, force-of-nature guy, yet so calm and soft-spoken that we thought surely the cardiac event must have been minor. He and Edie lived within a couple of blocks of the best hospital in the area, and we were comforted to think that Mike was so quickly in the hands of the finest physicians.

Neither Gerda nor I had showered, but because I wake each day with epic bed hair, looking not unlike Christopher Lloyd playing Doc in *Back to the Future,* Gerda urged me to shower while she joined Edie at the hospital. Later, when I got to the hospital, Gerda would come home to shower and then return.

By the time I showered but before I dressed, Gerda phoned me and, shaken by grief and in tears, said, "It's too late, he's gone."

After calling Linda to give her the terrible news, I left

Trixie in her office and drove to the hospital in a light rain.

Mike was so highly regarded and well liked by so many people that even though he was gone, more than a few wanted to come to the hospital to see him one last time, as there would be no viewing at a funeral home. Weeks later, hundreds would attend his memorial service, where I delivered a tribute to him and served as a kind of MC to introduce others who wished to speak. One of the hardest things that I have ever done was maintain my composure through that event, which God helped me to do for more than an hour, until I lost it at the very end.

On the morning that Mike died, we stayed at the hospital with Edie, her son, Eric—whom Mike had raised since he was a young child—with Mike's brother, Jeff, and Jeff's wife, Judy, to help greet those who had expressed a determination to come.

Gerda went with me to the holding room to spend a few minutes with Mike, and we were the better for having visited the body. In the face of one deceased, not prettified by a mortician's hand, you see the awful dignity of death, the transience of all things that requires of you absolute humility. You see as well the truth and the hope of life best expressed in the first and last lines of T.S. Eliot's "East Coker," part of *Four Quartets*: "In my beginning is my end . . . in my end is my beginning." I am born to die, but I trust that I die to live again.

That afternoon and far into the evening, many of

Mike's friends, his son, Jeff, and family members gathered with Edie at their house. We all brought far too much food not only for the practical reason that even mourners must still eat but also because such gatherings are two parts grief, two parts condolence, and one part gratitude to be among the living, which a lavish spread of food best expresses.

When we got home that evening, Trixie did not greet us in her usual delirious fashion. No wiggle this night, no happy panting. Her tail wagged but not exuberantly. She was eager to cuddle, as always, but more subdued.

I have said that she preferred to sleep in her dog bed, but I have saved for here the fact that during her seventh and eighth months with us, she decided that our bed was preferable after all. Trix slept at the foot of the mattress, so quiet through the night that we hardly were aware of her presence. At the end of the two months, she changed her mind, returned to her dog bed, and did not come back to ours again, except when the night was rocked by thunder and except for two other nights, of which this evening of Mike's death was one.

Certainly, dogs read our mood from a thousand telltales that we do not recognize in ourselves. They may even read us with something like a psychic perception. Trixie's demure behavior might have meant nothing more than that she sensed our grief and our solemnity. But I think dogs know.

I spent a large part of the following day with Edie and Eric. We went to the mortuary to make arrangements for the cremation. We went to my attorney—as they were currently without one—to discuss some legal issues regarding the estate, which the government, in its compassion, wants to see addressed before the bereaved can yet think clearly, and we talked through other issues that would need to be addressed. All this was complicated by terrible weather, a downpour of such intensity as to suggest the End of Days. And it was made worse by the bleak storm light, which robbed the day of color and dimension, and flattened our already low spirits.

After returning Edie and Eric to their place, on the way back to Harbor Ridge alone, I thought of what it would feel like to be returning to our house if Gerda had gone from it forever. And putting these memories on paper, the same dread inevitably settles over me. We have lived under one roof more than twice as long as we lived without each other before our wedding. The world never made sense until we were together, and I can't see how it would make sense if I had to live without her. There are moments, more of them in recent years, when the world appears to be descending into a hundred kinds of madness, when the sane life we have made for each other is more precious because it seems ever more rare and quaint in this age of unbelief, discontent, and irrationality. Solipsism, the strange conviction that only one's self is real, does not afflict me, but I can believe that if Gerda were to die before me, she might prove to be the last real thing, so that I and all the world around me would at once be colorless and without dimension.

•

That night, with rain beating on the windows, dinner for two and a bottle of wine by candlelight was a greater comfort than any king could derive from all his power and riches. Under the table, lying on my feet, Trixie was again subdued, and also later when she slept just this one more night at the foot of our bed.

Three days later, under a blue sky, we went to the construction site for a meeting with a few craftsmen and tradesmen who had long been on the project, to determine how we would finish what remained: a handful of simple interior items, some areas of hardscape and additional landscaping. For years, Mike's office was in a trailer on site, but some time ago he moved into a room in the service building at the back of the property. We would have to clean out his desk and files, separating his personal items from documents pertaining to our house. But this was not the day for that depressing task.

We were to meet with the interested parties in front of the service building, to tour the exterior of the house and compile a checklist of the remaining work. Since the driveway and walk-in gates had been installed, we could leave Trixie off her leash to enjoy the grass, in the shade of the California live oaks and pepper trees. When everyone had gathered, Trixie was not with us. She usually didn't wander out of sight, and we were concerned.

Someone reported having seen her moments ago around the door of the service building. I went looking for her and found her in Mike's office, standing at his chair.

Recalling this moment, I can easily go too far attempting to deduce her thoughts and feelings, and so it's best not to imagine them at all. She was just a dog, standing where Mike could often have been found on the phone, negotiating with suppliers and chasing down overdue orders of urgently needed items. She had thought to go there for some reason, and logically you could say she expected to find Mike, who always gave her a chest rub or a scratch behind the ears.

I watched her, waiting, and something more than expectation of a chest rub held her there, for she delayed another minute or two. The logical assumption is that memories held her, memories of Mike. But it seems memories would have held her only if she realized the sad context in which she considered them, and indeed her solemn mood seemed to confirm an appreciation of context. At last she turned her attention to me, and I said, "Let's go, Short Stuff."

She hesitated, surveyed the room again, and came to sit before me, head tilted back, ears raised just at the occiputs. This is as much as goldens are able to raise their pendulous ears, but it cubes their cuteness. I went to one knee and massaged her face with my fingertips and then with my knuckles, a pleasure she rated second only to food. Usually she closed her eyes during this boon, but now she held my stare. When I finished the face massage, she led the way out of the office, out of the building, into the sunshine.

Dogs know.

One day, before we adopted Trixie, as I came down the back stairs, I heard pitiable wailing, which at first sounded like a young child in misery. The cry might have been as near as the family room or living room, but soon I found the source outside. The neighbors kept two Alaskan malamutes, and one of them was sitting in the fenced run alongside their house, howling in distress. His cries were the most pathetic I had ever heard from an animal, yet no injury or product of illness was apparent.

The neighbors often had one or both of the dogs in the house, and they were not negligent. If they had been home, they would have heard this wailing and would have been examining the dog to determine its complaint.

When I went back inside to ask Gerda if she had a cellphone number for the people next door, we could hear the cries even in her office, which was at the farther side of the house from the afflicted animal. Gerda knew that no phone call was necessary. A short while earlier, she had encountered the neighbors in the street and learned that they were on the way to their veterinarian because one of their dogs was failing fast and needed to be put to sleep to spare it suffering.

The remaining malamute had often been alone in the run and had not howled. This was the anguished wailing of a grieving creature who knew his friend would not return. For three hours, he cried. After a silence, he cried again at twilight. For more than a month, this pathetic dog held forth two or three times every day, for an hour or more on each occasion. Never before or since have I heard such sorrowful, despairing cries, and nothing could console him.

And so dogs mourn.

We have all read the stories of nursing-home dogs that suddenly lavish even more affection on a patient who is apparently no more ill than previously but who passes away within the day.

And so dogs console.

In 1858, a shepherd known as Old Jock was buried in Greyfriars Abbey churchyard, in Edinburgh, Scotland. The next morning, his Skye terrier, Bobby, was found sleeping on his grave. Regardless of the weather, Bobby returned to keep a vigil every day for almost fourteen years. Visitors from around the world came to see this loyal terrier, and a monument to Greyfriars Bobby still stands in Edinburgh. Church officials allowed Bobby to be buried next to Old Jock.

And so dogs mourn not just the immediate loss but also the enduring memory of what was lost.

In AD 79, Mount Vesuvius erupted, destroying Pompeii, burying it under volcanic ash. Centuries later, excavators discovered a dog, Delta, whose collar described how he had saved his owner's life three times. Delta's body was lying over a child he had tried to protect from the volcanic horror.

If dogs were incapable of grasping the concept of mortality, they would make no effort to save us from death. If they understand that *we* are mortal, they surely know the same about themselves.

Skeptics have a reason for wanting to deny that dogs are aware of their mortality. Such an awareness, like an accurate awareness of time and its role in our lives, is a higher order of thinking than mere instinct, which is only pattern programming. Yet because dogs are acutely aware of death before they witness it, the concept has not been learned. Therefore, the knowledge is native to their minds, and we call such knowledge intuition.

For more than a century and a half, elite intellectuals have pressed upon us theories that try to reason us out of our native knowledge, to encourage us to deny that intuition exists. They are hostile to intuition, but not because by intuition we know that we are mortal or because by intuition we understand the basic past-present-future workings of time, or because by intuition we know that the whole is greater than any of its parts.

They are hostile to intuition because, as thousands of years of civilization will attest, we are born with a tao, a code of virtuous conduct, a sense of right and wrong, which is ours intuitively. This tao, which we all share, is the foundation for every great religion but also of every great culture that has ever given its people long periods of peace and stability under law, and also of every rational humanitarian impulse and project. If we recognize the existence of this tao, we cannot believe that life is meaningless, and we cannot succumb to nihilism or to cold materialism. If we recognize this tao, we may well accept the existence of the soul, whereafter we will not cooperate with those intellectuals who, in the modern age, have been in mad rebellion against all of human history that preceded them.

When we acknowledge that dogs are well aware of their and our mortality, we acknowledge they have intuition. From the skeptic's point of view, this is dangerous because it inspires us to regard our dogs with greater enlightenment, whereupon we may see that dogs, by intuition, also have a tao.

We have seen dogs slinking under a weight of guilt after they have turned the daily newspaper into confetti or chewed a slipper from which they were previously warned away. We have seen dogs in a state of shame, as Trixie was when she crawled on her belly and pressed her face into a corner after peeing on the carpet—even though the fault lay with me. We have seen dogs grin and prance with pride after performing a task as they were trained to do, which is a proper pride in the virtue of cooperation. When dogs risk their own lives to save one of us, they reveal their native knowledge expressed by Saint John in these words: "Greater love hath no man than this: that he lay down his life for his friends."

If we have been reasoned out of a belief in our intuition and therefore in our mind's native knowledge of wrong and right, we might wake from our trance of nihilism and discover that, after all, life does have meaning. If our dogs have a tao, we must have one, too, because dogs would not love us so much if we were nothing but meat machines without principles or purpose. Like human beings, dogs can be imperfect judges of characters, but they can't be wrong about *all* of us.

Most of us will never be able to live with as much joy as a dog brings to every moment of his day. But if we recognize that we share a tao, we then see that the dog lives closer to that code than we do, and the way to achieving greater joy becomes clear. Loyalty, unfailing love, instant forgiveness, a humble sense of his place in the scheme of things, a sense of wonder—these and other virtues of a dog arise from his innocence. The first step toward greater joy is to stop fleeing from innocence, begin retreating from cynicism and nihilism, and embrace once more the truth that life is mysterious and that it daily offers meaningful wonders for our consideration.

Dogs know.

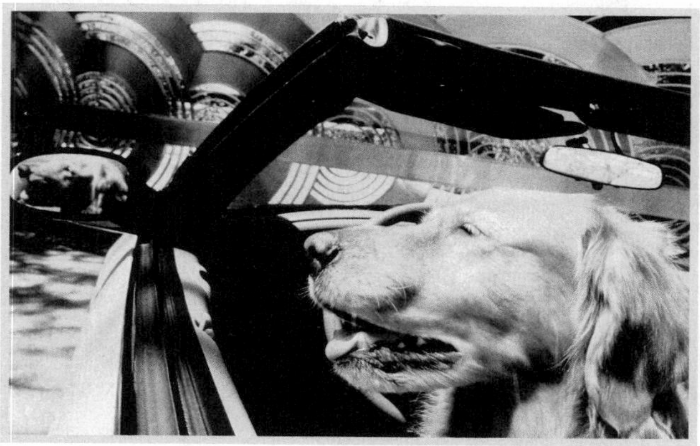

XVIII
elbow surgery and meatballs

TRIXIE BEGAN SECRETLY limping. I stepped out of a room and caught her hitching along the hallway as if she were auditioning for an all-canine version of *The Hunchback of Notre-Dame.* Crossing the bedroom, Gerda happened to glance back at Trix and saw that she was favoring her left forelimb. When she knew you had stopped to watch her, she made the effort to walk normally.

We checked her paw first, searching for a wound or an embedded splinter, but found nothing. After that examination, she made a heroic effort to avoid being caught in a limp, walking without hitch or hobble for the rest of the day.

Soon, however, she couldn't conceal that her left leg troubled her. Bruce Whitaker X-rayed her and suggested she might have the same congenital problem in her left elbow that, in her right elbow, forced her into early retirement from her assistance-dog duties.

A surgeon was recommended. On our first visit to him, he led us out to a service alley and asked me to walk Trixie thirty feet away and then back toward him while he watched how she moved. "Elbow," he declared.

He reached between her hind legs, feeling her pelvic bones. Then he suggested that I feel there as well and tell him what I found. Not having attended veterinary school, I considered myself inadequately educated to offer a second opinion or even a first. And I began to wonder about the surgeon's credentials, too, because he had said the problem was the elbow, which was at the other end of the dog from the pelvis.

Because he was wearing a white lab coat, possessed an air of authority, and resembled Ernest Hemingway, I did as he instructed. Hemingway drank the equivalent of a fifth and a half of booze every day, frequently went through six bottles of wine with dinner, was a notorious and perhaps pathological liar, and behaved monstrously to nearly everyone who befriended him, so I'm not sure why a resemblance in this case impressed me. Yes, at his best, Hemingway could write like a wizard, but so can David Mamet, whom I would nevertheless forbid to operate on my dog.

I felt at once that the left pelvic bone was thicker than the right. Trixie had been compensating for elbow pain for a long time, continuously shifting her weight backward, stressing the pelvis on that side until it thickened. Yet she had only begun to limp a few days ago.

In the examination room, the surgeon manipulated the elbow joint, trying to make Trixie whimper. When he told me what he was doing, I wanted to pick up a surgical clamp and work on his nose until *he* whimpered, but I restrained myself. He needed her response to confirm his diagnosis, because this kind of congenital disorder didn't always show up clearly on an X-ray.

Trixie refused to whimper. She didn't wince or start anxiety panting. She just smiled at me while the doctor forced her elbow into uncommon positions.

"She's a very stoic little dog," he said.

I had heard that comment before.

IN FEBRUARY OF that year, Trixie had been bitten by a German shepherd that I am convinced was a trained attack dog. She reacted to the bite as if it had been no more than a kiss.

On a Sunday afternoon, we were out for a walk. As always I had a little canister of pepper spray. I carried it in my right hand.

We turned a corner and started up a sloped street we had often walked before. A boy of about nine hung by his arms from a tree limb in a front yard to our right. He looked as innocent as a choirboy, but as we drew closer, something about his attitude suggested there would be black candles on any altar where he served.

Two steps farther, I saw what the property wall at the adjacent house had concealed during our approach: a huge German shepherd lying in the yard, back from the tree in which the boy did his monkey act. It was not on a leash or restrained by anything.

German shepherds are beautiful, affectionate, and intelligent. Regardless of the breed, however, when you see a loose dog large enough to pull a Honda, caution is wise.

The shepherd glanced at us, seemed disinterested. Nevertheless, I turned Trixie around and walked away, telling myself discretion was the better part of valor, though wondering what might be the better part of cowardice.

I had gone maybe eight steps when the boy called out, "Yeah, you *better* run."

We were walking, not running, but I wasn't going to get into an insult contest with a nine-year-old, especially not with a nine-year-old backed up by a 150-pound sabertooth dog. I could always have my revenge when it suited me, lie in wait for him some morning on the route he took to school, beat him up, and take his lunch money.

The kid's behavior so appalled me, however, that I stopped, gave him my best look of disapproval, and asked, "What did you say?"

He had said it once. He wasn't in a mood to repeat himself. He spoke instead to the German shepherd, something like, *"Get 'em!"*

The shepherd charged.

The day was warm for February, the trees swayed hypnotically in a mild breeze, and until this point in the walk, I felt a bit drowsy. Nothing brings you as fully awake as quickly as a giant dog that seems intent on getting a bite of your testicles.

As I aimed the pepper spray, I shouted, "Back!" and "Stop!" The shepherd heeded neither command, and I saw that he was charging not me but Trix, and that his trajectory would take him to her throat. So I squirted him.

The stream splashed into his nose and spattered across his face. He changed course but didn't turn entirely away. He seemed to bite Trixie on the left flank, just forward of the hip, and then he turned away and raced back toward the boy, sneezing.

Fortunately, I didn't assume the dog had been dissuaded, because sure enough he looped around and charged again. This time, the stream caught him in the eyes, which according to the instructions that came with the canister was the ideal hit. He turned away when he was six or eight feet from us.

He charged again. The third stream splashed his eyes, and once more he arced away from us.

Eerily silent through all this, the shepherd launched a fourth charge, this time straight at me because I had been such a bastard to him.

There were supposed to be five squirts in this canister. The shepherd retreated after taking the fourth stream in the face, and I wondered what I would do if he had not one but two more charges in him.

It might be cool to have the nickname Pegleg, and without a nose, I might have fewer sinus problems, but I really hoped not to end up with a high-pitched Mickey Mouse voice.

The shepherd had enough. He returned to the lawn where he was sitting before Hermann Goring IV sicced him on us, and he rubbed his face in the grass, trying to wipe off the noxious spray.

The kid was wide-eyed and speechless, and I had one more squirt in the can, but I decided to save it for the shepherd in case he got his second wind.

Trixie smiled at me and wagged her tail, and I felt like her knight in shining armor as I hurried her away from Dogzilla. We turned right at the corner and went four blocks on the next street before I stopped to examine her side where I thought the shepherd had bitten her. I couldn't find any blood, and I didn't want to linger. As we walked home, I glanced over my shoulder all the way.

I told Gerda about the encounter and showed her where the shepherd had seemed to nip Trixie. This time, when Gerda pulled back the thick fur, we saw the bite. The wound was barely bleeding because he had ripped off a patch of her skin the size of a silver dollar without getting his teeth into the meat of her.

•

This can't have felt like any kind of kiss. Yet Trixie never yelped or whimpered.

On Sunday, our vet's offices were closed. We rushed Trix to the emergency clinic near the airport. After the vet on duty sewed up the wound and gave us medication instructions, she said, "She's a very stoic little dog."

Short Stuff weighed over sixty pounds, but she was thoroughly feminine and appeared smaller than she was. She seemed particularly fragile to me as I lifted her into the back of our Explorer for the trip home from the clinic, because I couldn't stop thinking that the attacking shepherd might have gotten his teeth in her throat if the first blast of pepper spray had missed his muzzle.

I had no animosity toward the shepherd. I felt sorry for him, though I knew the spray caused only temporary misery. The dog had done what the boy had told him to do and what the boy's parents had evidently trained him to do. The people were the villains here, and the shepherd could, in a sense, be seen as a victim of theirs.

I reported the bite to animal control. The officer on the phone asked for the address. I told him the street name but did not know the house number. He *did* know the number, however, and knew the breed of the dog before I told him. Our attacker had a history.

Because I believe policemen and animal-control officers usually do a commendable and thankless job, I'm sorry to say the owners of this animal weren't fined and weren't issued even a warning citation, as far as I know.

After weeks of "investigation," an officer gave me an incoherent explanation of why the case would be closed without action.

Another officer, dismayed by the department's failure to act, told me that the owner of the shepherd had tight ties to the city government and was destined to skate until the dog one day drew blood from a person instead of from another dog. I thanked him for his off-the-record frankness, but I told him that my Trixie *was* a person. Being a dog lover himself, he understood what I meant.

"A VERY STOIC little dog," the joint surgeon said again.

Having been unable to get a whimper from Trixie when he flexed and stretched her elbow, he X-rayed it from different angles and was able to show Gerda and me the problem. Trix needed the same surgery on her left elbow as she had undergone on her right.

A couple of days later, we returned with her to the hospital. She would be staying overnight because surgery was at five o'clock in the morning. We took one of my dirty T-shirts to leave with her, so she'd have my familiar scent, and one of her favorite toys.

This was June 2000, after she had been living with us for a year and nine months. She had long ago ceased to be just a dog and became our daughter, too. Because she couldn't understand that hospitalization was for the best, leaving Trixie there felt like a betrayal. Gerda and I half wanted to go home and scourge each other with brambled branches as penance for not insisting on sleeping in the hospital-kennel cage with her.

At home, we split a bottle of wine with dinner, and I had an extra glass from a second bottle. My consumption was laughably low by the standards of Hemingway, but if Trixie had too many more health crises, I'd be pounding it down like Papa.

We were told that Trixie would have to stay at the hospital at least one night after the surgery, possibly as many as three. But the following day, the surgeon called twice, first to report that the operation had gone well, and later, at five o'clock, to tell us that we could bring her home.

"She's the calmest dog I've ever seen," he said. "She's made no effort to worry the incision, she isn't straining at her tether or barking, and yet she's been on her feet and alert hours sooner than usual."

When we arrived at the hospital to collect our girl, concerned parents crowded the waiting room. A few appeared haunted, and I knew that with their animals, they were facing worse problems than we were with Trixie. Gerda and I felt grateful, relieved, and happy that the Trickster was coming home.

Then a nurse brought her out to us, and poor Trix was in sorrier condition than we expected. Her left arm, shoulder, and part of her flank were shaved. She tottered shakily with the assistance of the nurse. At first her face remained hidden in the plastic Elizabethan collar—or cone—that prevented her from chewing at the incision. She surveyed the crowded room, searching for us, and when we bent toward her, she tilted her head back, revealing that her eyes were bloodshot and her facial fur matted with tears.

She grinned when she saw us, and we cried. We didn't sob noisily like babies, didn't blubber, but hot tears sprang forth as if our eyes were showerheads. The sobbing, the face-wrenching anguish, the bitter thickness in the throat that makes swallowing difficult, the heaviness in the chest that is the weight of what was lost: All of that would come in too few years. This was a small taste of that, not an inoculation to prepare us to better handle grief—nothing can immunize against grief—but a reminder to cherish what you love while you have it, so that when it passes, you will have memories of joy to sustain you.

Gerda took off Trixie's cone and rode in the cargo space of the Explorer with her, holding her and reassuring her.

One of the greatest gifts we receive from dogs is the tenderness they evoke in us. The disappointments of life, the injustices, the battering events that are beyond our control, and the betrayals that we endure from those we befriended and loved can make us cynical and turn our hearts into flint on which only the matches of anger and bitterness can be struck into flame. Other companion animals can make us more human, but because of the unique nature of dogs—their clear *delight* in being with us, the rejoicing with which they greet us when we come home to them, the reliable sunniness of their disposition, the joy they bring to playtime, the curiosity and wonder with which they embrace each new experience—they can melt away cynicism and sweeten a bitter heart.

And there is the matter of their gratitude. When Trixie came to us, I expected her delight, her rejoicing, her sunniness, her joy and curiosity and wonder, but the remarkable and constant gratitude that dogs express for what we give them is arguably the most endearing thing about them. A bowl of kibble is a matter of routine, but a dog seems never to take it for granted. After food, after the gift of a new toy, after a play session or a swim, in the middle of a cuddle that gives dogs such bliss, Trixie turned those soulful eyes on you and all but spoke with them, or gave your hand a thank-you lick, or nuzzled her cold nose into the palm of your hand. As surely as dogs read us and, by countless telltales, know our moods and feelings, so we can read their telltales if we put our minds to it, and perhaps gratitude is the thing we see most often.

When we did anything that particularly pleased her, she searched through her pile of toys, selecting this and that one but discarding each after consideration, until after a couple of minutes she arrived at the perfect stuffed plush animal for her purpose. In moments like this, it was always a plush toy, never a tug rope or a ball. Having made her choice, she brought it to us and placed it at our feet, not to induce us to play, but to say, *This is one of my favorite things. I want you to have it because you have been so kind to me.* Then she settled down and sighed, and sometimes went to sleep.

The surgeon told us that Trix would need six weeks to recover from elbow surgery. During the first three weeks of convalescence, he wanted her to be crated day and night.

We understood the need to prevent her from running

or jumping, but we knew our free-spirited Trickster, who had rarely been crated and never by us, wouldn't do well in extreme confinement. Because our desks are large, U-shaped affairs, we got permission to contain her within the work space by barricading the end with a four-foot-high, sectional pet fence that could be arranged in any configuration.

She spent part of the day with Gerda, part of the day with me. At night, the sectional gate could be arranged in a square, to form a cage, in which we put her bed and her water dish, giving her much more room than a crate.

During the day, Trix didn't have to wear the head cone, not only because she remained under our constant observation, but also because Gerda invented a clever garment that discouraged licking or biting at the surgical stitches. She took apart a couple of her tube tops and resewed them into snugly fit leggings. Because the tube-top material was stretchy and sort of ribbed-quilted, the legging was easy to pull on and thick enough to provide protection, covering Trixie's shaved forelimb from pastern to upper arm. I'm not sure this would work with a dog less cooperative than Trix. I think the legging prevented her from worrying the incision in part because chewing through it was too difficult but also because she understood the purpose of it and wanted to please her mom. She looked totally fab, as well.

At night, we didn't trust in the legging alone, and we needed to put the head cone on her. Dogs despise the cone. It's uncomfortable and confining, but they also realize it makes them look silly and is an affront to their dignity. When the cone went on, Trixie accepted it first with an expression of exasperation but then with a pitiful look that said, *What have I done to you that I deserve this?*

The first three weeks following surgery, Trix was not supposed to do stairs. As our offices and the master bedroom were on the third floor of that Harbor Ridge house, I had to get her down to the front door, on the second floor, four times a day to take her outside to toilet.

Because the house stood on a narrow lot and because the stairs—especially the back ones—were steep, the architect included an elevator. It was small, perhaps five feet square, cable-driven rather than hydraulic. I'm not claustrophobic, and I don't have a fear of elevators, but I did not like that small, wood-paneled cab. The motor that drove the cables was bolted between rafters in the attic, and the entire assemblage rattled and creaked and groaned and even issued curious animal shrieks while in operation, as if in addition to the electric motor, a couple of apes were required to haul on the cables and were not happy about their job. Gerda refused to ride in it, period. Until Trixie's surgery, we used the lift only as a freight elevator, to move heavy boxes.

During Trixie's convalescence, Gerda broke her rule against taking suicidal risks in claustrophobic conveyances and, when I was not available, accompanied our golden girl on the harrowing journey between the third and second floors. Love conquers all.

At the time, Trixie was still shy of her fifth birthday

and feared neither fireworks nor thunder, nor anything. She didn't fear the elevator, either, but she didn't like it. The first few times she rode in it with me, she kept looking around, trying to discern where all the noises were coming from and what they might portend. Soon she figured out that most of the tumult arose from overhead, whereafter she watched the ceiling with the obvious expectation that a disaster of one kind or another would at any moment befall us.

After half a week, riding down four times and up four times each day, Trix began occasionally to balk at another confinement in that contraption. When I opened the door, she sat down in the hallway in what we called her "bucket-bottom" posture. She weighed little more than sixty pounds, but when she parked her butt and did not want to enter that elevator, she might as well have weighed as much as a bucket full of lead shot. She was immovable.

I could lure her into the elevator with a tasty cookie, but that seemed deceptive. I could hope to outwait her—although she had the patience of Job, while I had the patience of a two-year-old. I could scold her, but considering her condition, I didn't have the heart for that. Besides, she was right: The elevator was a coffin-size *Titanic* on a vertical voyage to an iceless doom.

We reached a compromise. On one of our four daily trips, now and then on two of them, I carried her down and up the stairs, and the rest of the time, she rode without pulling the bucket-bottom trick on me.

The surgeon specified that she should walk only a hundred feet to and from each toilet during the first two weeks, two hundred feet during the third week. I tried to explain Trixie's toilet tao, but I saw by the look in his eyes that he heard the shrieking violins that accompanied the slashing knife in *Psycho*. I imagined being committed against my will to a mental ward where inevitably I would find myself in the company of X, who would have a list of a thousand people to whom I should send free books and invitations to party at our beach house. I said, "Yes, sir. A hundred feet. No problem."

Using a short leash, maintaining a slow pace, I walked Trixie to the neighbor's yard, an extra fifty feet. Otherwise, she would have tried to hold in her poop for the duration, and eventually we would have had a catastrophe that would make a plummeting elevator with screaming apes on the roof seem like a tea party.

In the fourth and fifth weeks, we were required to continue confining her, though she was allowed ten- and then fifteen-minute walks. Through the fourth week, Trixie endured these restrictions and indignities with higher spirits than I would have maintained in her situation, but then she fell into a depression. A depressed dog is more terrible than an epically constipated dog building toward a blow. They are by nature exuberant, merry creatures. We could not bear the sight of our elfin Trix so downcast that she spent the day in a sad-eyed listless detachment. Her tail didn't wag. No squeaking plush toy could engage her. When we rolled a ball to her, she let it bump against her snout and made no effort to seize it, evidently because she knew that she couldn't run off with it and tease us into pursuing her. Short Stuff was so disconsolate that even food couldn't rouse a grin from her, and she ate mechanically, without enthusiasm.

On Thursday, as we were coming up on our week-five Friday appointment with Trixie's surgeon, I called him to report on her mental state and to ask him to consider if we might be able to take her out to dinner with us on the weekend. I explained that there was a Swedish restaurant where the owners were dog lovers and welcomed us on their small patio. Trixie was fond of Gustaf, the partner who ran the front end of the business, and when we ate there, we ordered her a serving of little Swedish meatballs. We could park close to the place, lift her in and out of the Explorer, and walk her on a short leash. The patio was small and quiet, with little chance anything would happen there to excite her into injuring herself. Our girl needed a spirit-lifting excursion.

"That would be a bad idea," the surgeon said. "You should wait another week, until she's fully convalesced, and even then you're going to have to be cautious with her for a while."

Late Friday afternoon, when he examined Trix in his office, he spent more than the usual amount of time with her. He determined that her healing was further advanced than usual at the five-week mark. He relented, giving us permission to take her out to dinner that very night.

Giddy with anticipation, we raced home with her to give her a comb-out and to change our clothes. We couldn't wait to see her eyes light up when she recognized the restaurant, to see the grin that a dish of little meatballs would inspire.

I lifted her into the back of the Explorer again, and we set off into an evening full of promise. Trixie was lying in the cargo space, and Gerda was sitting in the backseat, holding the leash so Trixie wouldn't try to roam while in transit and perhaps be rocked off her feet.

A smart dog never stops surprising you with its sudden insights and the power of its perceptions. The trip to the restaurant involved four surface streets, a freeway, and another surface street, and we never followed that route to anything else. As I drove the first four streets and the freeway, Trixie lay in her depressive indifference, but when I followed the exit ramp and turned right on the fifth and final surface street, she startled Gerda by scrambling to her feet in the cargo space, pulling the leash taut. She looked out of the windows, left and right—and her tail began to swish.

"She knows where we're going," Gerda said. "How can she know?"

We were still more than a mile from the restaurant, but Trix grinned, panted happily, and used her tail as she had not used it in a week.

By the time we reached our destination and parked, every muscle in her body was tensed. She faced the tailgate with such anticipation that she seemed to be saying, *Open the darn thing or I'm going right through it.*

In spite of her excitement, she allowed herself to be

lifted out and gently set down. Then, as if propelled by her rotating tail, she strained to the limit of her leash and led us past the main entrance to the restaurant, along a promenade that served an open-air shopping plaza, and around to the patio on the back of the establishment.

Gustaf greeted us, lavished attention on Trixie, and led us to a table overlooking the promenade. When Gerda and I were served our first course, Short Stuff received a dish of the miniature meatballs.

For the rest of the evening, she either sat at the railing that encircled the patio or lay with her chin on the bottom horizontal and her face between two staves, watching with interest as people—and a few dogs—strolled past on their way to and from the shops. Her tail did not continuously move in broad sweeps, but it never fell entirely still, either. The tip of it twitched, twitched, twitched, because she knew that her long confinement was over and that soon she would be allowed to go on long walks and to play again. She had her life back, life was good, and she was never depressed thereafter.

All breeds of dogs have a sense of smell much greater than that of any human being, some of them merely thousands of times greater, some tens of thousands. It's possible that Trixie caught a thread of scent unique to the Swedish restaurant even when we were a mile away from it and even though she was inside an SUV.

Researchers once concocted a complex odor in a lab and taught a bloodhound to react to it in a specific fashion. Then they took the hound to the bottom of Manhattan Island, while others on the team traveled to the upper end of the borough, thirteen miles away. At the top of Manhattan, at a prearranged time, the researchers pulled the stopper out of a bottle of the laboratory-brewed stinky stuff and saturated a cloth with it. They waved the cloth in the air. They had chosen a day when a breeze moved north to south across the island, and they clocked the wind speed with anemometers at both the upper and lower locations. Less than a minute after the breeze should have carried the singular scent from one end of the island to the other, through one of the largest cities in the world, through millions of people and through a miasma of uncountable smells, the talented hound detected it and reacted to it, although the molecules must have been widely dispersed by air currents.

Trixie was no bloodhound. However, originally bred to work with hunters, golden retrievers are blessed with a sophisticated sense of smell. The restaurant was only a mile or so away, not thirteen miles, and a only few thousand people, not many millions, occupied the territory between our SUV and the restaurant. She might have snared an unraveling ribbon of scent from the air.

But I suspect that the other and no less amazing explanation is the correct one. We'd taken her to that restaurant by the same route on at least thirty occasions, and at the end of each fifteen-minute journey, she had received a dish of miniature meatballs. I think she learned that series of right and left turns and the approximate times between each turn, and associated that pattern of travel with the meatball treat. Her eruption out of listless depression into tail-wagging delight at the *instant* that I turned right onto the last street in the route is too meaningful to discount.

Or maybe she just read our minds.

XIX

"may i tell you a wonderful truth about your dog?"

THE SECOND NOVEL I wrote after Trixie came to us was *From the Corner of His Eye,* a massive story, an allegory that had numerous braided themes worked out through the largest cast of characters I had to that time dared to juggle in one book. The central theme around which the others wound was expressed by a character in the novel, a black minister named H. R. White, in a famous sermon of his, and I used part of that sermon as an epigraph prior to chapter one:

> "Each smallest act of kindness reverberates across great distances and spans of time, affecting lives unknown to the one whose generous spirit was the source of this good echo, because kindness is passed on and grows each time it's passed, until a simple courtesy becomes an act of selfless courage years later and far away. Likewise, each small meanness, each expression of hatred, each act of evil."

I don't work with outlines, character profiles, or even notes. I start a novel with only a premise and a couple of characters who intrigue me. Therefore, I was daunted but also exhilarated by the prospect of *showing* that theme, that truth, in dramatic action, which is what a novel must do—show, not tell. The task seemed immense, but after leaping into new territory with *False Memory,* I learned that the more overwhelming a project seemed to be, the more *fun* it was, as well.

The day I started *From the Corner of His Eye,* Gerda walked Trixie, combed her, and brought her to my office. After the you're-as-sweet-as-peaches-this-morning tummy rub, Trixie curled up on her bed in my office—she had beds in six rooms—and watched me from the corner of her eye as I ransacked my mind for the opening lines of the new book. An hour later, I had a first chapter unlike any that I had ever produced previously, and I wondered if some heretofore unrecognized sinister and self-destructive part of my mind might be setting me up for failure. The opening made a series of narrative promises that seemed impossible to fulfill:

> Bartholomew Lampion was blinded at the age of three, when surgeons reluctantly removed his eyes to save him from a fast-spreading cancer, but although eyeless, Barty regained his sight when he was thirteen.
>
> The sudden ascent from a decade of darkness into the glory of light was not brought about by the hands of a holy healer. No celestial trumpets announced the restoration of his vision, just as none had announced his birth.
>
> A roller coaster had something to do with his recovery, as did a seagull. And you can't discount the importance of Barty's profound desire to make his mother proud of him before her second death.
>
> The first time she died was the day Barty was born.
>
> January 6, 1965.
>
> In Bright Beach, California, most residents spoke of Barty's mother, Agnes Lampion—also known as the Pie Lady—with affection. She lived for others, her heart tuned to their anguish and their needs. In this materialistic world, her selflessness was cause for suspicion among those whose blood was as rich with cynicism as with iron. Even such hard souls,

> however, admitted that the Pie Lady had countless admirers and no enemies.
>
> The man who tore the Lampion family's world apart, on the night of Barty's birth, had not been her enemy. He was a stranger, but the chain of his destiny shared a link with theirs.

Eyes removed yet sight regained? Caused somehow by a roller coaster and a seagull and love for his mother? His mother, who died twice? I had no idea what any of this meant or how I would deliver on these bizarre narrative promises. One of my favorite reviews of the novel appeared in the *San Diego Union-Tribune,* where the critic said in part: "His opening is like a man announcing he will juggle bowling balls while frying eggs and piloting a hot-air balloon. Preposterous—but Koontz then proceeds to do it, and much more." He described accurately my concern as I sat in my office, reading that first chapter over and over. A hot-air balloon, indeed.

Over the years, when a story took a seemingly illogical or an incomprehensible twist, I learned that my subconscious or maybe my intuition was at work and that I should trust it. Eventually, the story would evolve to a point where the twist made perfect sense, and I was always amazed that on some level I had known all along what I was doing even while doubts bombarded my conscious mind.

But *From the Corner of His Eye* would have the most complex set of themes and the largest cast of characters that I had ever tackled. And now it opened with what appeared to be narrative promises highly difficult if not impossible to fulfill.

The more I observed Trixie, however, the more confident I felt about being able to write this challenging book. The protagnosists of *Corner* were people who suffered pain and terrible losses but who refused to embrace cynicism and who strove either to work their way back toward a condition of innocence or (in the case of the children in the cast) tried to hold fast to their innocence in a corrupted world. My revelation that Trixie's intelligence and sense of wonder revealed that she had a soul and the revelation that the innocence of her soul was the source of her constant joy prepared me to write convincingly about Agnes and her son, Barty. Junior Cain, the vicious yet hapless antagonist, embodied the fourth revelation I received from watching Trixie: that the flight from innocence so characteristic of our time is a leap into absurdity and insanity. Not only had Trixie prepared me to write this book, but she also had at least in part inspired it.

Because Trixie restored my sense of wonder to its childhood shine, I decided that having composed the first chapter, I *had* to write this story because I couldn't rest until I knew what had happened—and would happen—to blind Barty and to his mother.

FROM THE CORNER OF HIS EYE took a week short of a year to write, and by the middle of 2001, I was deep into another novel that proved no less complex and would wind up nearly as long, *One Door Away From Heaven.* On a working Saturday, I delayed Trixie's afternoon feeding by half an hour, until four o'clock, and then knocked off for the day. After she inhaled her kibble, finished licking her chops, and returned to the bowl to be certain she had not missed a kibble or two, we set out on an hour-long walk.

When you walk a dog regularly in the same community, you develop a group of acquaintances who are walking their dogs, too. Often you stop and chat for a couple of minutes, usually to swap dog stories, to talk about dog parks and dog beaches and dog treats and dog toys and dog illnesses and dog doctors and dog books and, you know, just dogs in general.

Most of the time, the other people don't ask your name and don't volunteer their names, not because they are obsessed with privacy but only because it doesn't cross their minds that our names matter in this particular social network. We are dog guardians, and that's usually all we need to know about one another, because we *do* know the names of one another's dogs.

Every time I encountered a new person with a dog I had never seen before, that person's first question to me went like this: "She's a beautiful golden. What's her name?" I introduced Trixie, complimented the newcomer's dog, and asked its name. If the dog's name was Sparky, the man walking him was known to me thereafter as "Sparky's dad." When Gerda came home from a walk with our girl, I'd ask if she met anyone, and she'd say, "Pookie's mom recommended this cafe that allows dogs on the patio, and Barney's dad says they have some fabulous new plush toys at Three Dog Bakery."

Reading the newspaper at breakfast one morning, I saw a photo of a couple we met sometimes on our dog walks. They had been given some community-service award. A day or two later, I remembered the article and said to Gerda, "Gizmo's dad and mom do a lot of good work for at-risk kids, got this award, photo in the paper."

Gerda said, "What're their names?"

I stared at her blankly.

She said, "Surely the paper didn't just refer to them as 'Gizmo's dad and mom.' "

"The story didn't even mention Gizmo," I said. "Which goes to show you how worthless most newspaper articles are. They never get the *real* story."

I am sure I read those people's names. I just didn't retain them because I already knew them as Gizmo's mom and dad, and that told me the most essential thing I needed to know for the limited social context in which we related to one another. If during daily walks you encountered a guy without a dog but with a third eye in his forehead, and if later at dinner you told your spouse, "I ran into Three Eyes this morning, had a nice little chat about designer sunglasses," the dinner conversation would not be significantly enhanced if you knew his real name was Jim Smith.

After encountering the same woman—Wally's mom—two or three times a week for over three years, during walks with Trixie, she crossed the street to me one morning, leading Wally, and said, "I owe you an apology. I didn't realize who you were."

"I'm Trixie's dad," I replied.

She said, "I've been reading your books for years, I love them, I've seen your pictures on the jackets, and for some reason I just didn't make the connection."

We chatted about books for a minute or two, and then I asked her name, since she now knew mine.

"I'm Wally's mom," she said, and we both laughed, and then she told me that Ralph's Supermarket had finally restocked Frosty Paws.

Ten minutes after we parted, I realized she hadn't answered my question. I still didn't know her name.

I am quite sure that at home that evening, she said something to her husband like: "I asked Trixie's dad when he has a new book coming out, and he said next month."

In Harbor Ridge, in addition to people walking their dogs, Gerda and I frequently encountered the grandfather of an Indian family who lived on the next block. He required the assistance of a walker, one of those models with wheels, and he proceeded at a slow but steady pace across the flat streets on top of the ridge, venturing out twice a day for what must have been a one-mile constitutional each time. I was impressed by his commitment to remaining active.

He had a round, merry face and a warm smile, and his slight musical accent was charming. And he always wanted to reach down and stroke Trixie's head while we exchanged pleasantries about the weather or about something in the news.

One day, as Trixie and I approached him, he said, "May I tell you a wonderful truth about your dog?" I said that nothing would please me more, and he said, "Perhaps you know what she is. Do you know what she is?"

Assuming he wanted to know her breed, I said, "She's a golden retriever."

"Yes, she is," he replied, "but that's not what I mean. In our religion, we believe in reincarnation. We live many times, you see, always seeking to be wiser than in our previous life, wiser and more virtuous. If we eventually lead a blameless life, a perfect life, we leave this world and need not endure it again. Between our human lives, we may be reincarnated as other creatures. Sometimes, when someone has led a *nearly* perfect life but is not yet worthy of nirvana, that person is reincarnated as a very beautiful dog. When the life as the dog comes to an end, the person is reincarnated one last time as a human being, and lives a perfect life. Your dog is a person who has almost arrived at complete enlightenment and will in the next life be perfect and blameless, a very great person. You have been given stewardship of what you in your faith might call a holy soul."

The grandfather's voice and manner were enthralling, and his comments about Trixie were so kind and sweet that I thanked him and said we'd always thought she was special. He said, "Tell your wife what I have told you," and I assured him that I couldn't wait to tell her and would do so as soon as I got home.

This might seem strange, but I walked a block before it occurred to me to connect his words to the incident in which I told Trixie that I knew she was an angel masquerading as a dog, and to the night that she seemed to take a tour of the upstairs with a presence invisible to me. A not unpleasant chill traveled my spine.

As a Christian, I do not believe in reincarnation, but I believe there was something unique and significant about Trixie. Many people recognized that uniqueness and expressed their perception of it in different ways. Frequently, when we were on a restaurant patio with Trix, other customers, having watched her during dinner, stopped by our table to say a word about her, and more often than referring to her beauty or to her good behavior, they said, "She's really special, isn't she?" We always said, "Thank you. We think she's very special." But after the grandfather told me what he believed her to be, I was more than previously aware of how often the word *special* was used to describe her.

Our friends Andy and Anne Wickstrom, whom we had known since my college years and who grow more interesting—or maybe just more strange—year by year, came to stay with us for a week in our new house. They were taken with Trixie, and she with them, and the five of us had a grand time. A month or so after they had returned home to the East Coast, we were chatting on the phone, and

Anne said that they had tried to tell friends about Trix, to convey how special she was, but eventually realized that words and anecdotes simply were inadequate to make anyone fully understand Short Stuff's magical personality and appeal.

Writing this memoir, I have come up against that wall many times. I have had to accept that although I have done my best to paint this portrait of her, I am incapable of doing her justice. The ineffable cannot be described. A mystery is a mystery precisely because it has not been solved, and some mysteries are insoluble.

In that second novel written after Trixie's arrival, *From the Corner of His Eye,* I brought closer to the surface those spiritual issues that had underpinned some of my previous books: that the world is a place of mystery and purpose, that science—especially quantum mechanics—and faith are not antagonistic to each other but are in fact complementary, that we are a community of potential saints with a shared destiny and each of us is a thread in a tapestry of meaning. When it was published, it received more generous reviews than could be squeezed into the first five pages of the subsequent paperback edition. That was lovely, but reviews are not as satisfying as reader response. In its first eight years, *Corner* has sold six million copies worldwide and has generated tens of thousands of letters from readers, some of the most intelligent and moving mail I have ever received.

I dedicated *Corner*: "To Gerda. In the thousands of days of my life, the most momentous was—and always will be—the day we met." I had dedicated other books to Gerda, but with this novel, I finally felt that I'd written one worthy of her.

Five years later, I dedicated a book to Trixie. By then, in my slow and thickheaded way, I had at last fully realized how much she had changed not only me but my writing.

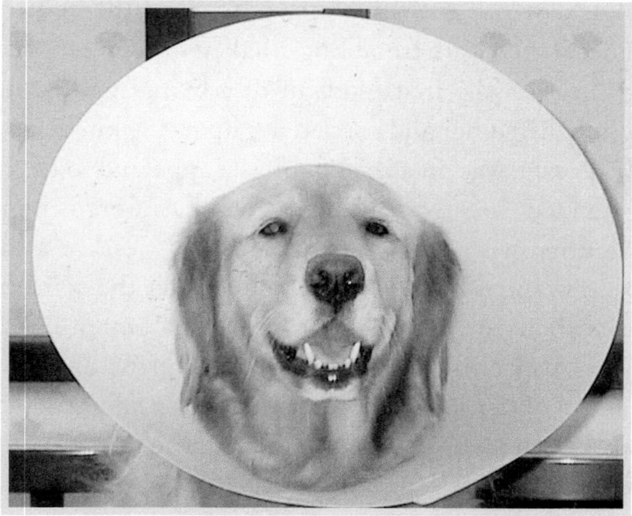

XX

dr. death and dr. berry

ONE EVENING, AFTER we had moved into our new house, Trix and I went to the backyard so she could pee before bed. Inside once more, as she preceded me up the back stairs, eager for the cookie she would receive from her kitchen stash, she suddenly let out a thin but sharp yelp, a single fraction-of-a-second cry, and froze with her back legs and forelimbs on different steps. She turned her head to stare at me with alarm. I could not persuade her to lift a single paw. She seemed prepared to stand there forever, and her flanks were trembling. Shaken by a presentiment that this was the first moment of a living nightmare, I carefully lifted her and carried her up to the kitchen.

When she was on a level floor, she appeared to be fine. She padded directly to where her cookies were kept and favored me with one of her you-know-I-deserve-a-treat looks. I wanted to believe the moment on the stairs had been without serious meaning, but I knew better. Fearing for her, suspecting that one kind of suffering or another lay ahead of her, I gave her three cookies and would have given her the whole jar if she hadn't turned away after three and gone to her water bowl.

We rode up to the master suite in the elevator, avoiding the stairs. This was a larger, more modern, and more professionally installed elevator than the one that we had in the previous house. Instead of clattering up and clamoring down on cables, the cab was on the end of a hydraulic ram that raised and lowered it quietly, without any shrieking apes in the attic. Trixie had no reservations about riding in it.

To spare Gerda from a sleepless night, I didn't tell her about the scary moment on the stairs until morning. After breakfast kibble, when I took Trixie out to toilet, she had difficulty getting her bowels started. She squatted, began to strain, immediately stopped and crabbed forward, tried again, stopped, crabbed forward, as if the straining caused her discomfort. Finally she managed to do her business.

I took her to her vets at the animal hospital, and they X-rayed her spine. The preliminary diagnosis was that Trixie had a spinal problem and would need to undergo an MRI before it could be determined whether she required surgery.

We made an appointment with a veterinary surgeon who had the best references. After two days of avoiding stairs, we took Trixie in at five o'clock in the morning for an MRI. We were told that we could pick her up twelve hours later, at five in the afternoon. This seemed an inordinately long time, but they explained that she needed to be fully recovered from sedation before they would release her.

At five o'clock sharp, when we returned, a veterinary assistant brought Trixie out to the reception lounge. Our girl was in shocking condition. She wobbled when she walked, and her legs repeatedly went limp under her, dumping her on the floor. Her lower eyelids were so prolapsed that her thoroughly bloodshot eyes looked as if they would roll out of the sockets, and they were weeping copiously. She did not appear to recognize us, neither wagged her tail nor responded in any way when we touched her and spoke to her.

We knew that the veterinary surgeon was still in the facility because we heard the receptionist speaking with him on the intercom. Gerda told the vet assistant that we wanted to see the doctor, but the doctor declined to come out and speak with us.

Although she is petite and soft-spoken, Gerda can put a steely menace in that gentle voice without raising it.

The vet assistant backed off a step when Gerda said, "He won't come out? This dog has been grossly oversedated. Where is he? We'll go to him."

By the alternately defensive and aggressive—and entirely inappropriate—reponses of some on the facility staff, we suspected that scenes like this had occurred before. After originally telling us they would not release Trix until she was completely recovered from anesthesia, they now insisted there was nothing to worry about if we took her home even though she couldn't stand up and didn't know who we were.

No doubt the doctor had skedaddled out a back exit, and we would get no satisfaction even if we kicked open every door in the place to track him down. Trixie was our first priority. I carried her to our SUV, and we took her home.

Expecting that she might vomit or void in some other way, we bedded down, all three of us, on the kitchen floor, where we were close to whatever we might need: cold water, ice, all the cleaning materials in the nearby laundry room, an outside door. Trix seemed as unable to sleep as she was unable to walk. Lying on makeshift bedding with our girl between us, we stroked her and spoke softly to her, worried that she had suffered permanent brain damage by reason of reckless over-sedation, and we worked up the kind of quiet rage that usually leads to shotguns and Molotov cocktails.

Near midnight, Trixie was finally able to rise far enough to lap some water from a bowl. She started dozing on and off, but she showed no sign that she recognized us until four o'clock in the morning, eleven hours after we brought her home. She was not fully herself until around five o'clock the next afternoon, *twenty-four hours* after we brought her home from Dr. Death's Hospital of Horrors.

Adding a rotten cherry to this toxic sundae, Dr. Death's office called to inform us that the MRI had not produced sufficiently clear images to make a diagnosis. I wanted to know what combination of illegal drugs the doctor himself used on the average day, but his staff was reluctant to disclose this information.

I TOOK TRIXIE next to a neurosurgeon, Dr. Wayne Berry, who came into the examination room, at once got down on the floor with Short Stuff, called her "Cookie," and won her adoration in about one minute flat. He had taught veterinary surgery at South Africa's largest university, but he had immigrated to the United States with his family some years earlier. He was ex-military, with the rational self-confidence, air of competence, and efficient manner of a man who knew the value of discipline and who had a sense of honor about how he lived his life and performed his surgery.

Wayne wanted another MRI. He assured me that it would provide a definitive diagnosis because he would be present during the procedure and would insist on redoing any slice of the image that wasn't clear. I needed to return with Trixie by five thirty Wednesday morning.

I explained the condition in which Trix had been delivered to us by Dr. Death. Wayne guaranteed that when he met with me at eleven thirty to deliver the diagnosis, she would be recovered 100 percent from the anesthetic.

Wednesday morning, when I took Trixie down in the elevator to the lowest floor of the house without stopping at the kitchen, on the main level, to dish up her breakfast kibble, she hesitated at the door to the garage, waiting for me to realize my mistake. When I said, "Let's go," which was not just a suggestion but a command from her CCI training, she favored me with the Ross look. I explained that because of the anesthesia, she could not have any food in her stomach during the test, lest she regurgitate and aspirate vomit into her lungs or choke to death. If I say so myself, I have a talent for illuminating complex concepts for the edification of dogs, employing pantomime and sound effects to define and supplement the words they might not know. My aspirating-vomit illustration would have made Dustin Hoffman weep with envy. Trixie still gave me the Ross look and seemed to be on the verge of a bucket-bottom move.

I resorted to what always works when all else fails in these situations. Squirming with pretend delight, I spoke in a voice breathless with excitement, words tumbling over one another: *"Let's go to doctor! Trixie go, doctor, doctor! Holy moly, fun, fun, Trixie, Dad, doctor, fun, fun! Play dog doctor game, fun, fun! Go, go!"* Dogs are strongly food oriented, but if they think a great good time is being had somewhere and they can be part of it, they will accept a delay in mealtime in order to get to the party.

Considering how well dogs read us the rest of the time, I'm surprised how reliably this cheap trick can whip them into a state of excitement and distract them even from breakfast. I would think once in a while the dog might realize, *Waaaait just a minute. The last time there was going to be a holy-moly-fun-fun-go-go thing, I ended up with a needle in my arm, a cone around my head, and a thermometer up my butt.* Their perpetual readiness for play is endearing, and their willingness to forgive deception time after time is one of the key differences between the heart of a dog and the human heart.

Trixie bought my wriggling, breathless promise of fun. She allowed me to lift her into the SUV, and as we drove off into the still-dark morning, she panted at the windows, anticipating a grand adventure.

I felt like scum. Not the worst kind of scum. Not the kind of scum you'd scrape off a kitchen floor in Hell. I felt like the kind of scum you sometimes find on the skin of a tomato that's two days past overripe, but that was bad enough.

We arrived at Dr. Berry's facility early, just as the mobile MRI arrived aboard an eighteen-wheeler. The truck was so huge, it looked like the transport that a villain in one of Roger Moore's James Bond movies would use to haul around a doomsday weapon in search of the most visually exciting landscape in which to have a chase scene.

Trixie pranced to the reception desk, and the women

there cooed and fussed over her. After giving me an I'm-all-right-Dad look over her shoulder, she went with a veterinary assistant through a swinging door, where she would not find the promised party.

At home, with more than five hours to kill before we would have our girl back and hear what surgery she might require, I could not concentrate to write. I could pass the time doing correspondence, a mountain of which looms constantly in a writer's life, or I could spend the morning sulking in an armchair, looking through magazines, and binge-eating cookies. By cookies, I mean the human kind, not the dog kind; this was not a self-punishing Freudian guilt-fest. As I stuffed myself with cookies, I *did* to some degree consider it a form of penance for deceiving the Trickster: *If I keep this up, I'm going to be gross, I'm going to be as disgusting as Jabba the Hutt, the Beautiful People of Newport Beach will recoil from me in revulsion, and that's exactly what I deserve. Okay, no more of those regular chocolate chip. Time for some of the chocolate chocolate chip.*

Gerda and I met with Dr. Berry at eleven thirty. He clipped the MRI pictures of Trixie's spine to the display board and asked if we could see the problem. The images were so crisp and clear that even Dr. Death might have been able to see the problem, assuming sobriety. Our girl's spine was revealed as an exquisitely regular series of black and white forms—until near the base, the pattern compressed, deteriorated. One of the spaces that allowed a spinal nerve to pass freely from the spinal cord, between the vertebra and spinous process of vertebra, was drastically narrowed by excess bone that pinched the nerve.

I hasten to say that I'm not necessarily describing Trixie's condition in correct medical terms. I didn't ask Wayne Berry to proof the previous paragraph. I want to convey how his explanation sounded to me, an ignorant layman alarmed by even the most benign medical terms like "intravenous injection" and "Band-Aid," because it made my heart heavy with worry. Spinal conditions, I thought, frequently brought with them the possibility of paralysis.

Short Stuff could not climb stairs without pain. Lately she had not been in a mood to chase a tennis ball, obviously because of the pinched nerve. At every toilet, she made multiple attempts at a bowel movement, awkwardly and repeatedly crabbing forward in her squat before at last making a successful effort, because straining at stool stressed the affected nerve. She required surgery to grind away the excess bone and allow the nerve free passage.

Gerda looked grim when she asked what might go wrong during such a procedure, and Wayne was admirably direct and succinct. If damage occurred to the spinal nerve during surgery, Trixie's back legs might be paralyzed for life. Or she might be incontinent for life. Or both paralyzed and incontinent.

He gave us a moment to absorb those possibilities, and then with a quiet confidence that had about it no slightest quality of a boast, he said, "But neither of those things has ever happened to an animal when I've done this surgery."

As we scheduled the procedure, they brought Trixie to us, fresh from her MRI. The difference between her condition after surviving Dr. Death and her condition after going through the same test under Wayne's care could not have been more dramatic. She was wide-awake and delighted to see us. She needed neither pantomime nor sound effects to convey to me how much she wanted the breakfast that she had been tricked out of seven hours earlier.

Wayne said, "In her condition, she'll have moderate to severe discomfort through a wide range of motion. But you say she only cried out that once on the stairs."

"And maybe once when she was chasing a ball the day before," I remembered. "It was a thin, sharp sound, very brief. At the time, I wasn't even sure it was Trix. But it was similar to the sound she made when she froze on the stairs."

He shook his head. "She's a very stoic little dog."

I nodded because I could not speak. When we have the deepest of affection for a dog, we do not possess that love but are possessed by it, and sometimes it takes us by surprise, overwhelms us. As quick and agile and strong as a dog may be, as in harmony with nature and as sure of its place in the vertical of sacred order as it may be, a dog is vulnerable to all the afflictions and misfortunes of this world. When we take a dog into our lives, we ask for its trust, and the trust is freely given. We promise, *I will always love you and bring you through troubled times.* This promise is sincerely, solemnly made. But in the dog's life as in our own, there come those moments when we are not in control, when we are forced to acknowledge our essential helplessness. To want desperately to protect a dog and to have to trust instead in others—even a fine surgeon—compels us to yield to the recognition of the limits of the human condition, about which we daily avoid consideration. Looking into the trusting eyes of the dog, which feels safe in our care, and knowing that we do not deserve the totality of its faith in us, we are shaken and humbled.

Again I think of lines from "East Coker" by T. S. Eliot: "The only wisdom we can hope to acquire / Is the wisdom of humility."

Within a couple of days of her second MRI, Trixie underwent spinal surgery. No complications ensued. She was neither left paralyzed nor incontinent, and she had no more pain.

She needed three weeks to convalesce, half the time required when she had surgery on the elbow joint. She couldn't reach the dorsal incision, which meant she didn't have to wear a cone.

Because I was working on a deadline to complete *Odd Thomas,* Trixie's care fell mostly to Gerda through those three weeks. *Odd Thomas* is a novel about perseverance in the face of terrible loss, about holding fast to rational hope in a world of pain, about finding peace—not bitterness—in the memory of love taken by untimely death.

Trixie's back was decorated with twenty-nine steel sutures, like a long zipper in a dog suit. I called her Frankenpuppy. She didn't think that was as amusing as I did.

This surgery gave her years more of a high-quality life,

during which she fully enjoyed the fenced acreage of our new house. As any dog is remarkably grateful for each kindness it receives, Gerda and I were grateful for every day this joyous creature graced our lives. The only wisdom is humility, which engenders gratitude, and humility is the condition of the heart essential for us to know peace.

XXI

critic, author, dog entrepreneur

OUR NEW HOUSE has a home theater with a large screen. The first time we settled there to watch a film, a Sandra Bullock comedy, we were surprised when Trixie leaped onto the seat beside Gerda's before I could sit down. Trix took advantage of furniture privileges only where they were given; and we had not extended them to the theater.

Instead of telling her to get down, we granted privileges after the fact. She looked so cute sitting erect in a theater chair. And we were intrigued by her apparent eagerness for whatever experience might be offered in this strange new room.

I sat beside Short Stuff and pretended that I knew what I was doing with an array of touch-screen controls more complex than the cockpit panel in a 747. Much to my surprise, the lights dimmed, red-velvet curtains drew aside, and the movie appeared on the screen.

Warmed by a flush of pride, I told myself that if I could master *this,* then I might one day figure out how to use the coffeemaker. I have always had big dreams.

We assumed that after a few minutes, Trixie would become bored with the movie and get off the chair. Five minutes passed, ten, and she remained riveted by the images on the screen.

Gerda and I repeatedly looked past Trix, raising our eyebrows at each other, amused by her devotion to Sandra Bullock's comical problems almost as much as we were by the—quite good—movie.

Perhaps the size of the images or the clarity of the projection transfixed our girl. She remained in the chair during the entire movie. Except for two five-minute periods when she chose to lie on the seat and rest her chin on the chair arm, she sat upright. And even in the down position, she kept her gaze on the screen.

The second time we used the theater, we ran another comedy, and again Trixie watched it beginning to end, sitting in a chair between her mom and me. I half expected her to ask for popcorn.

Instead of another comedy, we ran an action film on the third visit to our theater. We were eager to see it because some critics called it cutting-edge, maximum cool, and said the lead character was "a James Bond for the new and much hipper millennium." The movie was *XXX,* starring Vin Diesel, and those critics had probably called *Dumb and Dumber* an intellectual triumph.

Again, Trixie sat between Gerda and me, attentively watching the screen. For about four minutes. Then she got down, settled on the floor, and stuck her head *under* the chair. She remained there for the remainder of the film, a more perceptive critic than those who had touted *XXX.*

In recent years, if a film didn't shine in the first fifteen minutes, we knew from bitter experience that it would be a rusted tangle of junk to the end, and we gave it no more of our time. That worked for a while, but we began to resent those wasted fifteen-minute blocks of our brief sojourn on this world, which could have been better spent hanging by our thumbs.

Yet we were so convinced the praise we read for *XXX* could not be entirely half-baked that we sat through the whole dismal thing, expecting brilliance to burst from the screen at any moment, stunning us both emotionally and intellectually. Trix, head under her chair, must have been thinking, *Do I know these people? What has happened to their judgment? What are they going to force me to watch next*—Old Yeller, *when the dog gets whacked?*

In subsequent years, she never returned to a theater chair. When we watched a film, she sprawled on the floor and dozed. If we had not destroyed her love of movies by running *XXX*, perhaps she would have become a major director.

SOME OF THOSE experts who always make my brain itch tell us that dogs can't see and/or make sense of images on a television or a movie screen because they haven't the brain power to imagine the third dimension that is missing from a two-dimensional image.

In our previous house, we watched movies on the big-screen TV in our family room. Usually, I sat on the floor, with my back against the sectional sofa, so I could give Trixie a long tummy rub and ear scratch.

The screen was much smaller and the image less clear than what we would have eventually in our theater in the next house, but from time to time, Trix seemed to take an interest in the story. If she happened to be watching when a dog entered the frame, she stood and wagged her tail. It was the image that attracted her, because she reacted even when no bark or doggy panting alerted her to a canine presence in the film. Cat actors interested her more than canines. She had been raised with cats and liked them.

One evening, a character rolled into a scene in a wheelchair, which electrified Trixie. She stood and watched intently, and even approached the screen for a closer look.

I'm sure she remembered a time when a person in a wheelchair needed her, and when she served ably.

She was not an assistance dog anymore, but a princess, and she wished to be treated as one. Even when watching a movie, I was expected to properly revere her.

I learned not to sit on that family-room floor in my bare feet. If Trixie thought I had gotten too interested in whatever was on the screen and that I was giving her less attention than she deserved, she slipped out from under my massaging hand and went to my feet to lick my toes and distract me from the movie. The first time she tried this, I was determined to tough it out, imagining that she would stop the tickling if I didn't laugh, if I remained intent on the screen. Judging by how quickly she reduced me to giggling hysteria, I would not long resist spilling my guts if waterboarded.

LASSIE IS MORE famous than Trixie, but I must note that Lassie never wrote a book, whereas Trixie has now written three for adults and two for children. So there.

Kate Hartson, Trixie's first publisher, likes dogs. She is nuts about dogs. As far as I can tell, she knows nothing about current events, and I suspect that if she caught a TV news report that Earth was on a collision course with a massive asteroid, she would say, "Yeah, all right, I'll worry about that later, right now it's time to run on the beach with the dogs!" She talks more about her dogs than she does about her husband, Bill, and he doesn't seem to mind.

"The dogs are more interesting than I am," he once said. They have had a series of stunningly beautiful German shepherds bred and trained by the Monks of New Skete.

At one time, I worked with Kate when she was at Random House. She is charming, enthusiastic, and always full of ideas for new ways of publishing. Eventually she founded Yorkville Press, and while casting around for books to publish, she contacted me to ask if I had any ideas. I suggested a volume on Canine Companions for Independence and introduced Kate to the folks at the Oceanside campus. Eventually she published a beautiful book on CCI, *Love Heels,* that included a couple of hundred wonderful full-color photographs, and I wrote a foreword for the project.

With my encouragement, Trixie had been writing pieces for our snail-mail newsletter and Web site. Kate saw these and suggested that we do a book by Trix, with lots of photographs, with her humorous observations about life, in her doggy voice. Following is one of the pieces that inspired Kate to think Trixie could be a successful author.

My Summer

by Trixie Koontz, Dog

Dad teaches me to type. Hold pencil in mouth and type. At first is fun. Then is not fun. He says to me, "Write, Trixie, write. Write essay for Web site." Being good dog, I write. Not fun, but I write. Expect treat for writing. Get no treat. Stop writing. Get treat. Carob biscuit. Good, good, good. Okay, so I write some more.

Dad promises Web site visitors my essay end of July. Must give up important ball chasing, important napping, important sniffing—all to write. Work hard. Writing hard. So many words. Stupid punctuation rules. Hate semicolons. Hate; hate; hate. Chew up many pencils in frustration.

Finish article. Give to Dad. Then I rip guts out of duck. Duck is not real. Is Booda duck, stuffed toy. I am gentle dog. Cannot hurt real duck or even cat. But am hell on stuffed toys. Work off tension. Rip, rip, rip. Feel pretty good. Cough up soggy wad of Booda-duck stuffing. Feel even better.

Dad gives editorial suggestions. Stupid suggestions.

Stupid, stupid, stupid! He is not editor, is writer. Like me, Trixie Koontz, who is dog. I pretend to listen.

Am actually thinking about bacon. Bacon is good. Bacon is very good. I am good, too. People call me "good dog, good, very good." Bacon is very good. I am very good. But I am not bacon. Why not? Mysterious.

Then I think about cats. What is *wrong* with them? Who do they think they are? What do they *want*? Who *invented* them, anyway? Not *God,* surely. Maybe *Satan*? So nervous writing about cats, I use too many italics. Then I hit hateful semicolon key; don't know why; but I do it again; and whimper.

Dogs are not born to write essays. Maybe fiction. Maybe poetry. Not essays. Maybe advertising copy.

Here is my advertising copy: BACON IS VERY GOOD. BUY BACON. BUY LOTS OF BACON. GIVE TO ME. THANK YOU.

Dad gives me editorial notes for study. Eight pages. I pee on them. He gets message.

Dad says will give my essay to webmaster as is. Webmaster is nice person, nice. She will know good writing when she sees it.

Days pass. Weeks. Chase ball. Chase rabbits. Chase butterfly. Chase Frisbee. Begin to notice sameness in leisure-time activities. Pull tug-toy snake. Pull, pull, pull. Pull tug-toy bone. Pull, pull, pull tug-toy rope. Lick forepaw. Lick other forepaw. Lick a more private place. Still do not taste like bacon. Get belly rub from Mom. Get belly rub from Dad. Mom. Dad. Mom. Dad. Get belly rub from Linda. Get belly rub from Elaine. From housekeeper Elisa. Belly rub, belly rub. Read *Bleak House* by Mr. Charles Dickens, study brilliant characterizations, ponder tragedy of human condition. New tennis ball. Chase, chase, chase! Suddenly is September.

Webmaster asks where is Trixie essay? Where? Dad lost. Dad got busy working on new book, got busy, forgot fabulous Trixie essay, and lost it. My human ate my homework. Sort of.

•

> All my hard word, my struggle, so many hateful semicolons. All for what? All for nothing. Essay lost. All for nothing. Feel like character in *Bleak House*.
>
> Think about getting attorney. Get literary agent instead. Writing fiction. Novel. Maybe knock Dad off best-seller list. Teach him lesson. Writing novel called *My Bacon* by Trixie Koontz, Dog. Already have invitation from Larry King, David Letterman, be on shows, do publicity, sell book, get belly rub from Dave. Maybe get limo for media tour. Ride around in limo, chasing cats. Life is good when you're a dog.

Based on material like that, Kate believed a Trixie book would sell. I thought Kate might have lost her mind. Six years later, I'm still not certain of her mental condition, but in my mind's ear, I don't hear the shrieking violins from *Psycho* when she's around, just the eerie and disturbing music from *Twin Peaks*. Anyway, I agreed to work with her on *Life Is Good,* Trixie's first book, and on other books thereafter.

Kate came from New York to Newport Beach for three days with an extremely talented book designer, Tina Taylor, and an equally talented photographer, Monique Stauder, who eventually took almost 1,800 photos of our golden girl, including fantastic shots of her in the pool, swimming and aboard her float.

From the day we met her, Trix posed for snapshots,

and she had romanced the videocam when the *Pinnacle* crew showed up during her first week with us. But in those three days with Kate, Tina, and Monique, she revealed a patience and camera-awareness, no less professional than a top-ten model.

Because I couldn't always be present to oversee Trixie during the photo sessions, Linda filled in when I was busy. At one point, along the entry walk, where there were beds of vivid orange-gold flowers, Monique wanted Trixie to lie among the blooms. Linda was concerned about damaging the flowers, but she also knew that Trixie never went in the flower beds, as if avoiding landscape destruction were another rule of her personal tao.

Sitting patiently on the walkway, Trixie listened to this discussion, and then settled the issue by crossing to the flowers, lying on the pavement, and gently lowering only her head into the blooms, so she would not damage any plants. Monique seized the moment: Trixie's head, pillowed in the flowers—her eyes closed as if she is asleep and dreaming—is one of the most charming photos in *Life Is Good*.

On numerous occasions, Short Stuff seemed to understand what was being said, and she posed as Monique wished. The most impressive exhibition of this uncanny awareness occurred on the south lawn, when Monique wanted to get several photos of Trixie wriggling on her back, on the grass, with all four legs in the air. I was present, as were Linda, Kate, and Tina.

Monique had seen Trixie wriggling previously, when a camera was not at hand, and she assumed that I could get her to do this on command. I disappointed Monique when I explained that this was something dogs did of their own volition, when they wished, and I could not deliver such a performance with a word or gesture. No sooner had I said this than Short Stuff dropped to the lawn, rolled onto her back, and began to wriggle. Monique leaped at the opportunity and began to shoot pictures from various angles.

"How long does she do this?" Monique asked.

"Half a minute, a minute, never any longer," I replied.

"Oh, I want her with her head to the left, and she has it to the right, I wish she'd move it," Monique said.

Trixie turned her head to the left.

Monique got the shots she wanted, and then said, "I wish she'd stop moving, just lay on her back with all four legs in the air."

Trixie at once stopped wriggling and remained on her back, all legs in the air.

Kate, Linda, Tina, and I thought this was highly amusing. But then as Monique continued to express her wishes, moving around Trix, shooting from a standing position, then kneeling, and then lying on the ground, the dog did everything the photographer asked of her as soon as it was asked. We stopped laughing and fell into an astonished silence. Monique had been working with Trixie for a few minutes when I glanced at my watch and started to time the event. When Monique had taken every shot she hoped for, Trixie had been on her back, posing this way and that, for eight minutes. Add the three minutes that Trix clocked before I'd begun timing. *That,* we all agreed, was strange.

Trixie's *Life Is Good* went on to sell sixteen times as many copies as *my* first hardcover novel. She has since published two additional books for adults, a calendar, and has two children's books coming from Putnam.

The Trickster has become not only a busy author but also an entrepreneur. PetSmart, the national chain of stores, will have a two-month promotion of licensed products in the Trixie Koontz/Dog Bliss You line during July and August of 2009. We are in talks with other retailers about additional Trixie products, from toys and clothing to video games.

Short Stuff has become a conglomerate.

All author royalties and proceeds from the Trixie books and products are donated to the Trixie Fund at Canine Companions for Independence, which pays catastrophic veterinarian bills for the companion dogs of people with disabilities who cannot handle such large unexpected expenses. In 2008, seventy-one dogs received treatment that they might otherwise not have gotten.

Gerda and I break into smiles every time we think about what a long shadow this little dog has cast even after moving on from this world. And she has just begun.

Her books and other efforts are about laughter, love,

finding happiness, maintaining hope, achieving peace, earning redemption, and embracing the wonder and the mystery of this world. As *Reader's Digest* reported in its "Quotes" feature, Trixie believes, "Love and sausage are alike. Can never have enough of either."

XXII

endings always come too fast

OUR FRIEND CHRISTOPHER CHECK is a former marine, a devout Catholic, a writer, a speaker, a man of many talents, who crackles with so much energy that he makes my hair stand on end from a distance of forty feet. When he visited southern California to give the commencement address at St. Michael's School, which is a project of St. Michael's Abbey, Chris brought two Norbertine monks from St. Michael's—Father Jerome and Father Hugh—to our house for dinner.

I had corresponded with Father Jerome for a couple of years, but I had never met him. He generously wrote for me a lengthy account of daily life in a monastery, which was invaluable when I was writing *Brother Odd*.

When Chris burst through the front door, fortunately breaking no glass, Trixie scampered straight to him, greeting an old friend. By the time she got the attention she deserved, the house electrical system adjusted to Chris's presence, the lights stopped pulsing, and Trixie turned to the fathers, clearly fascinated by their radiant white habits.

Her reaction to these two visitors could not have been more different from her reaction to X. Wagging her tail, wiggling her entire body, she offered them her belly without hesitation. During the evening, she stayed close to the fathers, even to the extent that, as we stood talking in the front hall, she sprang onto a sofa on which she'd never before perched, so she could be closer to our level, and at dinner she rested behind their chairs when usually she would curl up near Gerda or me.

Knowing me so well, perhaps Trixie expected that when Father Jerome and Father Hugh stood up from the dinner table, their white habits would appear to have been tie-dyed. I must say *I* was most impressed when, at the end of the evening, those habits remained spotless.

Gerda and I and our three guests had a grand evening full of stimulating conversation and laughter. One high point occurred when Father Hugh said to Father Jerome, "What do you think of this dog?"

Father Jerome said, "She's special, mysterious in her way."

"We've heard that before," I assured them.

The Catholic church has a long intellectual tradition that has produced some of the most rigorously logical and beautifully reasoned philosophical works in Western culture. In their modesty, neither Father Jerome nor Father Hugh would ever claim to be an intellectual (and what a ragtag mob they would be associating with if they did), but they seemed to me to be intellectuals in the best—if not the most common—sense of the word, which includes humility and honor in its definition. Trixie inspired an interesting discussion of the proposition, explored in many writings about faith, that when the supernatural steps into time, into our world from outside of time, it does not work through dazzling wonders; instead, it manifests subtly, through elements of the natural world. Like dogs.

To us, Trixie was more than a dog. She was as a child, entrusted to our care, so that we might find in ourselves greater tenderness than we had imagined we possessed. But she was other than a child. She was an inspiration who restored our sense of wonder. She was a revelation who by her natural virtues encouraged me to take a new, risky, and challenging direction in my writing.

I am in fact the fool who, throughout this account, I have said I am, so you may make of this what you will: I believe that Trixie, in addition to being a dog and a child and an inspiration and a revelation, was also a quiet theophany, a subtle manifestation of God, for by her innocent joy and by her actions in my life, she lifted from me all doubts of the sacred nature of our existence.

T. S. Eliot again, in "East Coker," lays down a truth that both comforts and terrifies: "And what you do not know is the only thing you know." By "know" he means not our schooling as much as our learned convictions, the ideologies and fatuities and platitudes by which we define ourselves to ourselves and to others—and which are ignorance passing for knowledge. Such knowledge is of things that do not last, of systems that do not work, of pathways that lead nowhere. What we do *not* know—the destiny of the soul, the nature of eternity—is the knowledge that matters most, and only when we recognize this truth can we live with the humility required in the face of eternity.

What I do not know is the only thing I know, and in that paradox sits Trixie. I do not know what she was in the fullness of her being, other than a dog, but I know the effect she had on us, and I know that she was both flesh and mystery, and therefore I know that she was something more than I can know.

ON WEDNESDAY, JUNE 22, 2007, Trixie seemed listless, not her usual self, and I took her to the veterinarian. Bill Lyle thought she might have an infection, and he put her on an antibiotic.

Thursday, she seemed already to be more like herself. I hid each capsule of medication in a gob of peanut butter, and in return for the treat, Trix pretended to be fooled.

At eleven thirty Friday morning, Trixie refused food for the first time in her life, declining to take a single piece of the apple-cinnamon rice cake, one of her favorite things. Nothing could have been more ominous than this chow hound suddenly without appetite.

Bill Lyle had the day off, and I took our girl to see Bruce Whitaker. That afternoon, in an ultrasound scan, he discovered a tumor on the spleen. "It could burst at any time, and she'll die if it does. You have to get her into surgery right away."

A young vet tech, David, accompanied me to the SUV with Trixie, to lift her into the vehicle without putting pressure on her abdomen. He said, "Don't drive too fast, you don't need an accident. God is with her, you'll get there in time, she'll be okay."

His concern and kindness helped settle my nerves. On the drive to the veterinary specialty hospital, the facility at which Wayne Berry had performed Trixie's spinal surgery, I did not exceed the speed limit more than did the other traffic. But mine was not the slowest vehicle on the road, either.

In spite of not feeling well, Trix sat up in back, gazing out one window and then another. Regardless of the circumstances or the destination, a car ride was an adventure to be enjoyed.

The day was warm but not insufferably hot, the sky

cloudless, the air dry and limpid. The mountains rose purple in the east. This was a perfect afternoon for chasing tennis balls on the pepper-tree lawn, for sitting together on the outdoor sofa in the cool shade of the game-room terrace, watching hummingbirds hovering among the roses, the ocean in the distance. How much it hurt to think that this beautiful day was beyond our enjoyment now, and that perhaps all other days in the future would be less beautiful for the absence of her golden grin, her shimmering coat, herself.

Gerda had left the house on errands before Trixie refused her eleven thirty treat. She didn't know that the day had taken a dark turn.

Sometimes, when going places where she felt ringing cell phones would be an intrusion—we are old-fashioned in that regard—Gerda did not switch on hers. This was one of those times, and I couldn't raise her. I called Linda, told her what had happened, and asked her to track Gerda down and tell her to join me at the specialty hospital, which was in Irvine.

Trix and I arrived at the hospital shortly before four o'clock. When I led her to the front desk, she surprised me by standing on her back legs, putting her forepaws on the counter, and greeting the reception staff with a big grin. We occasionally called her Miss Sociable, and she was not going to let illness rob her of that title.

Because Bruce Whitaker had called ahead, Dr. Adam Gassel was ready to see her when we arrived. He came out to the waiting room to explain to me the couple of tests he needed to perform before surgery and to give me a very preliminary prognosis. He inspired confidence, much as Wayne Berry had done four years earlier, and I knew Trix was in good hands.

Gerda arrived, aware that our girl's condition was serious, but she didn't know how grave because I had not spelled it out in detail to Linda. Dr. Gassel thought there was a good chance that if this was cancer, it had spread to her liver. In spite of ultrasound scans, which had to be done, he would not know for sure how bad things were until he opened her to remove the spleen. In the kindest and most direct way—directness in such moments is the *essence* of kindness—he warned me that there was a possibility he would find cancer so widely spread that he would have to come out of surgery, leaving her on the table, so we could decide whether to close her up and revive her without taking further action—or end her suffering while she was already anesthetized.

Gerda said sharply, "Don't be so negative." She pressed her lips together because they were trembling. I realized that I should not have done an information dump on her. I had learned these details and possibilities in stages, and I'd had time to absorb them. She was hit with it all at once, which made hope harder to hold on to. And we both needed hope.

In the large waiting room, on a Friday evening, a few people came and went with their pets, but we were often alone. We sat side by side, sometimes holding hands, anchoring each other in the shallow optimism that circumstances allowed.

•

Wayne Berry heard that Trixie had been admitted. He came to reassure us that she could have no better surgeon for this procedure than Dr. Gassel. "She's a tough one, your girl. Never count her out. She'll stand right up from this." He hugged Gerda, then me, and reminded us how little fazed Trixie had been after spinal surgery.

Sometimes kindness can devastate, perhaps because we see so little of it day to day that we are unprepared for the way it pierces when we experience it in a time of crisis.

Alone again, Gerda and I tried to talk of other things than our girl, but nothing else mattered enough to be worth the words. So we recalled the best of those daily moments when Short Stuff made us laugh, and the memories could still raise a smile, though they also raised tears.

Between us, we demolished a box of Kleenex. We assumed some people must have thought we were a pair of basket cases—until we realized that five large boxes of Kleenex were distributed around the room. Anguish was common in that place.

We were told by staff that Dr. Gassel had opened Trixie, that the tumor had begun to burst, that a half liter of blood had poured into her abdominal cavity, but the situation had been addressed in time. The surgeon would report to us later, after he had closed her and assessed her recovery from anesthesia.

If I had gotten her to the specialty hospital an hour later, she would by now have died.

A bridge had been safely crossed. But a bridge to what?

•

We would not know, for sure, until the analysis of the tumor samples came back from the lab the following week.

At eight thirty Friday evening, Adam Gassel came to the waiting room. "She's doing well. Ultrasound suggested her liver and kidneys were clean, but I found nodules on the surface. They aren't uncommon in older dogs, and they don't necessarily indicate cancer."

The waiting had begun. Sometimes waiting is worse than knowing, and this was one of those times.

At home, we ate what we found in the refrigerator, but nothing had any taste, and we had little appetite. In bed, in the dark, we held hands for a long time and said nothing.

I never went to sleep that night, but spoke to God for hours. At first I asked Him to give Trixie just two more good years. But then I realized that I was praying for something that I wanted, which is not the purpose of prayer. My faith tells me that we should pray for strength to face our challenges, and for wisdom, but otherwise only for other people. And so I acknowledged my selfishness in wanting the joy of Trixie for two more years, and I asked instead that, if she must leave us, we be given the strength to cope with our grief, because her perfect innocence and loyalty and gift for affection constituted an immeasurable loss.

Adam Gassel called at nine in the morning with news. Trixie had gotten to her feet at four o'clock Saturday morning, only eight hours after surgery. She had a strong appetite. Her red-cell count wasn't what it needed to be. But if that issue could be resolved, she would still be going home Monday or Tuesday. We could visit her for half an hour around four o'clock that day, and again on Sunday.

We existed for four o'clock. At the specialty hospital, they brought Trixie to a consulting room, where we could lie on the floor with her. She was not herself, on painkillers that mellowed her to the condition of a bored sloth, but she was not as detached from reality as were most of the film producers and directors with whom I had worked over the years, and she recognized us. We cuddled her and were rewarded with a few thumps of her tail. They allowed us to stay not half an hour, but an hour and a half.

Her beautiful silky white ventral coat had been shaved off, her pink belly exposed. The sutured incision measured twelve inches, but I was in no mood this time to make a Frankenpuppy joke.

Gerda and I visited her again on Sunday afternoon, when she proved to be more like herself. We yearned to take her home, but while her red-cell count was better, her doctor still needed to monitor her closely.

In eight years and nine months, Trixie had been away from us only during the few nights that she previously spent in hospitals and one night that she visited with her aunt Lynn and uncle Vito. We had never boarded her. Now the house seemed empty and cold without our girl.

Monday morning, Dr. Gassel called to say the red-cell issue was resolved. We could bring Trixie home as soon as we wished. I arrived at the hospital half an hour later.

As I paid the bill, a couple of staff members reported that during her three-night stay, Trix made not one sound, neither a bark nor a whimper. Our stoic little dog. Because she was so calm, they decided not to keep her caged after the first night because they doubted she would strain her incision. She was allowed to socialize with the staff, as far as her leash would permit. Each time another dog whimpered, in fear or on the down slope of a med cycle and not yet scheduled for its next dose, Trixie went to its cage, lying near it, making eye contact, and inevitably the complaining dog quieted.

I recalled the grandfather with his walker: *"You have been given stewardship of what you in your faith might call a holy soul."*

When the paperwork was done and I had reviewed the instructions regarding her care and medications, they brought Short Stuff to me, and, oh, she was fully herself now: eyes sparkling, ears raised in expectation, pep in her step, tail waving hello to those whom she approached and thank you to those who were behind her.

I went to my knees and rubbed her face with my fingers, with my knuckles, as she liked. She made a rare sound: a catlike purr.

They put a cone on her head to prevent her from bothering her incision. She had made no attempt to lick or worry the sutures; but perhaps the ride in the SUV would make her nervous.

All the way home, she sat in the back, drinking in the

passing sights. I glimpsed her in the rearview mirror, grinning at me as if even the hated cone could not spoil this moment of reclaimed freedom.

At home, I freed her from the cone, for at all times, either Gerda or I, or both of us, would be with her. She greeted her mom with kisses and wiggled with delight on seeing Linda again. Elaine was retired, but the strange aura of Elaine still hung around her office chair, and the Trickster sniffed at that. She greeted Elisa, too, Krista, Jose, Fabian, and everyone else who worked with us and who smiled to see her prancing through the halls every day.

That evening I lifted her onto our bed. She knew this was the best place for her now, and she made no attempt to get down. The three of us were so happy to be together that we all slept soundly that night, past the hour at which for years we had routinely arisen.

We never put the cone on her again. She didn't chew at her sutures, didn't once lick the incision.

Although we had hope that the biopsies would come back negative, there seemed every reason to forget about keeping her weight at the ideal sixty-five pounds. In those days, Dannon made a non-yogurt, low-carb smoothie that I loved, especially the peach. I had sometimes shared a few spoonfuls with Trix. Now I poured an entire seven-ounce bottle in a bowl and set it before her. She looked at me as if I'd lost my mind, sharing so much of this ambrosia, but she set to work on it before I changed my mind.

Tuesday and Wednesday were good days, but on

Thursday, June 28, Dr. Gassel called with bad news. The tumor of the spleen, which he removed, was malignant, also the liver lesions, but the kidneys were not involved.

With the surgeon's guidance, we determined that chemotherapy would begin on July 10, the day Trix's sutures were to be removed. Ninety percent of dogs handle chemotherapy well, without the side effects that humans suffer.

That Thursday evening, we invited some neighbors to dinner, knowing that the best thing for Trixie would be people. Nothing excited her like the sound of the doorbell, because whoever came calling was her old friend or her new one—except for X. That was a fine evening for her, and she happily received the affection of all.

The next morning, Friday, a week after Trix's surgery, Gerda and I returned with her to the specialty hospital to meet the woman who would be her oncologist and to wait during an echocardiogram that would ascertain any problem, congenital or otherwise, that might limit the type and potency of the chemo she would receive.

They found another tumor in her heart. The cancer was called hemangiosarcoma, and her prognosis was grim. She would not be a candidate for chemo of any potency.

Worse, they discovered a blood clot on the wall of her heart. Were it to break loose, she would suffer a pulmonary embolism and die. Dr. Gassel could not say with certainty how long she would live, but he suggested two weeks.

In a state of despair, we brought her home, determined

to make perfect days of whatever time our golden girl had left. She was in no pain, following the splenectomy. The staples in her tummy would not allow her to run and jump, but she could have all other kinds of fun, including anything she wanted to eat, even ice cream by the dish.

Gerda and I could hardly bear eye contact with each other, as tears threatened each of us at the thought of the other's approaching loss. But we reached out more often to touch, to hold hands.

Our friends and neighbors Mike and Mary Lou Delaney, with their usual graciousness, gave us a harbor of love and understanding. "You don't want to be alone this evening," Mike said. "Come on down, nothing special, pizza and wine."

In the past, for the five of us, Mike planned short vacations in Rancho Santa Fe, at a splendid resort that was friendly to dogs. He arranged every detail, including searching out restaurants to which we could take Trixie. He'd recently planned a longer autumn excursion to Yosemite, though it would not happen now.

To simplify things, Mike prefers to drive every mile of the trip and to pay for food and lodging and everything else with his credit cards. After we're home, he copies receipts, gives us an accounting, and we send him a check for half. This is unbelievably convenient for me and Gerda. In fact, I now know what a kept man feels like—though in my adolescent fantasies, my sugar mama more resembled Marilyn Monroe than the rangy specimen that is Mike Delaney.

Mike is retired from a life in lubricants, which isn't half as racy as it sounds. The Delaneys owned a company that made a wide range of petroleum-based lubricants for industry. These days, Mike manages investments, worries about his grandchildren's future, and tries to keep Mary Lou out of trouble. The investments and the grandchildren get about 10 percent of that time.

Mary Lou was once a cheerleader back in the day, and I mean back in the day when the football was a rock and when the game had to be halted every time a mastodon ambled onto the field. She and Gerda became friends before I met Mary Lou, so there wasn't much I could do about it except commit suicide, to which I have moral objections.

Only a month before, my novel *The Good Guy* appeared with this dedication: "To Mike and Mary Lou Delaney, for your kindness, for your friendship, and for all the laughter—even if a lot of the time you don't know why we're laughing at you. With you. Laughing with you. We love you guys."

So that Friday evening, after receiving Trixie's grim prognosis, we took her with us to the Delaneys' house. Our girl especially loved Mike and Mary Lou, and roamed their home as though it were her own. We sat at the patio for a while, and Short Stuff explored every corner of their yard and garden, giving herself as fully as ever to the wonder of all things. Repeatedly, she came to us for a pat or pet, then returned to her explorations.

Mary Lou cooked a special chicken breast for Trix, and Trix found it delicious, along with other treats we had brought for her. She was as happy as we had ever seen—and that is a happiness of the highest order.

At eleven o'clock, we went home with the hope of two weeks of our girl's company. The crisis, however, came before dawn.

We woke to the sound of Trixie having breathing difficulties. She had wanted to sleep in her bed again, and now she sat beside it in a state of high distress. She labored for breath—but did not whimper.

We thought the moment had come, that a piece of the blood clot on the wall of her heart had traveled to one of her lungs. We dropped to our knees and held her, trying to comfort and reassure her.

During the following terrible half an hour, I feared for Gerda because she was shaking so violently with the prospect of our loss. Not merely her hands shook, but also her entire body, as though the temperature of the room had plunged below zero.

Having survived a rotten childhood, having survived a near-thing knife attack when I was forty-four, having seen a man shot in front of me and having looked down the barrel of that same gun, I had known what it felt like to be helpless in the face of mortal threat, but I had never before felt a fraction as helpless as I felt with Trixie wheezing in my arms. Here was the truth of our condition in this world, which we strive so hard to deny every day: Each of us, each living thing, lives by the hand of grace. I did not want to see our beautiful girl die in this manner, not with fear or suffering, yet I had no power to spare her.

I did not weep, and neither did Gerda. We would not distress her with our tears while she struggled to breathe. We prayed for strength, and strength was given.

After half an hour, Trixie abruptly recovered. She began to breathe normally. I dared to hope the blood clot had not traveled after all.

I asked Trix if she wanted to pee, for it was nearly the hour of her usual morning toilet. She responded at once, rising to all four paws. When she followed me from the bedroom, her tail was wagging.

We rode the elevator down to the ground floor. Walking the long hallway to the terrace and the terrace to the lawn, Short Stuff put on a brave show at my side, pretending to be free of all distress. As soon as she had finished peeing, however, her legs went wobbly, and she had no strength. Nevertheless, she made her way shakily from the lawn to the covered terrace, to the couch that was arguably her favorite place on the property.

This time she could not spring onto the furniture. I lifted her.

We often sat there for an hour at a time. Trixie liked to watch the birds and the wind in the trees and the roses swaying on their stems, while I petted her and rubbed the oh-that's-good spots behind her velvet ears. There were times she seemed willing to sit on that terrace for half the day, merely observing, marveling at the wondrous nature of all ordinary things.

Gerda brought a bowl of water in case it might be wanted, and we sat on the couch, with Trixie between us, from five forty in the morning until one o'clock in the afternoon. Our golden girl was listless but neither in pain nor afraid. The first time I offered her food, she wanted none. But the second time, she ate a dish of kibble and a tablespoon of peanut butter.

She wanted to be stroked and held, and to hear us tell her how good she was, how beautiful. Dogs come to love the human voice, which they strive all their lives to understand. In better days, when we sat in that same place, I made up silly songs about her, impromptu odes sung to some of my favorite doo-wop numbers. She grinned at me when I sang, and her tail thumped when she heard her name embedded in a melody.

Now it was clear that she had ridden down in the elevator and had found the strength to walk to the terrace because this was where she wanted to be when the end came. We expected her to pass at any moment, but she held on for hours, raising her head from time to time to look out at this place she loved: the broad yard and the roses and the sky curving down to the sea.

This was not only a Saturday, but also the first day of an unusually long Fourth of July holiday, and we worried that Trixie might have another seizure later in the afternoon or evening, when we wouldn't be able easily to get help. If it was not her fate to die suddenly, we could not let her suffer a prolonged passing. Shortly after one o'clock, I called Newport Hills Animal Hospital, and discovered that both Bruce Whitaker and Bill Lyle were off for the weekend; another veterinarian was covering the office. When I shared our situation with the receptionist, she told me that Bruce was at a tennis game and that she could reach him.

He called back within minutes. When I told him how Trixie had struggled for breath and described her current condition, he wanted to come to the house to see her rather than frighten her by having her brought to the office. Before one thirty, he arrived.

Trixie raised her head, grinned, and twitched her tail when I led Bruce out of the game room, onto the terrace. She submitted to examination with her usual grace. Bruce said she would probably die in the night or on Sunday at the latest. Although she was currently in no pain, she was weak, with low blood pressure and perhaps with internal bleeding.

"When it happens," I asked, "will she be in pain?"

"Possibly, yes," Bruce said.

"For a moment, for minutes, how long?"

"There's no way to know."

I asked him one more question that might have seemed odd to him, though he gave no indication that it was. "Will she cry out? Will she cry out in pain?"

"She might, yes."

In her life, this stoic little dog had endured serious physical maladies followed by four surgeries and four recuperations, without a single whimper or protest of any kind. If she cried out in pain and fear, her cry would shred my heart, and Gerda's. But it was not Gerda or me about whom I was concerned. I didn't want this brave dog, this creature of such fortitude and fine heart, to hear her own cry as the last sound she knew of this Earth. In her final moments, I meant to help her be what she had been during her entire life: an embodiment of quiet courage, unbowed by suffering.

Little more than half an hour later, at two o'clock Saturday afternoon, Bruce returned, carrying his medical kit. With him was a vet technician: David, who had advised me not to drive recklessly on my way to the specialty hospital eight days earlier, and who had said, "God is with her."

In my view, in the case of a human being, a natural death is death with dignity. Animals are innocents, however, and we serve as stewards of them, with the obligation to treat them with mercy.

So there on her favorite couch, on the covered terrace, where she could breathe in all the good rich smells of grass and trees and roses, we opened for her the unseen gate, so that she could walk again not on her now weak legs but on the still strong legs of her spirit, walk beyond that gate, an innocent into a realm of innocence, home forever. As her mom cradled Trixie's body and told her she was an angel, I held her sweet face in my hands and stared into her beautiful eyes, and as always she returned my gaze forthrightly. I told her that she was the sweetest dog in the world, that her mom and I were so proud of her, that we loved her as desperately as anyone might love his own child, that she was a gift from God, and she fell asleep not forever but just for the moment between the death of her body and the awakening of her spirit in the radiance of grace where she belonged.

XXIII

"in my end is my beginning"

LOVE AND LOSS are inextricably entwined because we are mortal and can know love only under the condition that what we love will inevitably be lost. That afternoon on the terrace, Gerda and I felt hammered by our loss, and broken.

Bruce Whitaker, whose work had brought him to many such moments, wept with us, as did David, who said, "She was such a very special dog." Later David would write us to say, in part, "Trixie had a special place in my heart. Normally, I am able to maintain a certain amount of detachment. In her case, this was simply not possible for me."

Together, Bruce and David wrapped Trixie in a blanket, and David carried her to the SUV in which they had arrived. Arms around each other, Gerda and I followed them through the downstairs and into the garage, where our golden girl's tail slipped from the folds of the blanket and trailed behind her, as if her spirit lingered just long enough to arrange this final farewell.

We could have buried Trixie on our property, but we didn't want to leave her remains there if the day ever came when we lived elsewhere. Her ashes will be with us wherever we might go. The pet cemetery that would conduct the cremation remained closed through Wednesday, for the long Fourth of July holiday. Bruce would keep her in his freezer until Thursday morning.

In the house once more, Gerda and I were lost. We didn't seem to belong there anymore. Every room was familiar yet as different as a room in someone else's house. We did not know what to do, did not want to do anything, but could not sit idle because, in idleness, the ever-pressing grief became crushing, suffocating.

Then Gerda was so shaken by the sight of one of Trixie's dog beds that she wanted to collect them all—many of them new—from every room, strip off the covers, wash and dry them, and put the beds away in a storeroom until they could be offered to employees and friends who had dogs. We gathered up the plush toys, as well, scores of them, because they were no longer merely toys but also needles in the heart.

All our lives, work had been our refuge and redemption. Now only work could prevent despair from overwhelming us.

I called Mike and Mary Lou Delaney, Linda, and only a few other people who knew Trixie best, who had spent much time with her and who thought of her as something more than a dog, though a dog itself is a glorious thing to be. I couldn't bear to call many people, because each time that I told the story of her death, I broke down as I had never done before. Gerda could speak to no one about it for days, to no one but me, and as so often in our lives together, we were for each other the rock that gave us footing.

We took comfort in the knowledge that God is never cruel, there is a reason for all things. We must know the pain of loss because if we never knew it, we would have no compassion for others, and we would become monsters of self-regard, creatures of unalloyed self-interest. The terrible pain of loss teaches humility to our prideful kind, has the power to soften uncaring hearts, to make a better person of a good one.

THE PET CEMETERY covered a considerable tract of land. Most of the hundreds upon hundreds of granite markers were decorated with real or artificial flowers, flags, dog toys, and balloons. Judging by these displays, this place was more frequently visited than any burial ground where human beings were interred.

The crematorium was in a garagelike structure behind the main building in which business and services were conducted. We were led there to see the body Thursday morning, because we wanted to be certain that Trixie's remains did not go into the fire with others.

During the half-hour drive from home, we steeled ourselves for the likelihood that this moment would be grotesque. After all, the body had been frozen since Saturday, had been brought here only this morning; it could not have fully thawed.

Instead of a grisly sight, we came upon a scene of stark truth and beauty. The crematorium was a plain rough space: dark rafters, chipped concrete floor, intricacies of shadows in the corners, hard light falling through the open door and directly upon the cremator, reality as Andrew Wyeth might have captured it in a painting. The cremator was a solid brute of iron and concrete, old and scarred by years of use, and the air smelled of a purifying heat. On a wheeled cart was a pallet, and on the pallet lay the body of our girl. Before the body was frozen, Bruce Whitaker or David had been so kind as to position it so that Trixie appeared merely to be sleeping, curled with her head resting on her paws. Her eyes were closed, her face serene. Her fur was cool and soft to the touch.

"She was so beautiful," Gerda said, "so beautiful," and in fact it seemed that this golden girl was more beautiful than I remembered, that only five days could steal from memory some of the full glory that was this dog.

During the first half of the 150-minute cremation, Gerda and I sat side by side on a couch in the waiting area of the mortuary. We paged again and again through *Life Is Good,* Trixie's first book, which contained so many photographs of her. In the cremation vigil, this was a way to celebrate her life.

Thereafter, we walked the cemetery, where the headstones were carved with expressions of love, devotion, and gratitude. In those grave markers were enough stories to keep a novelist in material for a lifetime.

We took the ashes home in a bronze urn and put the urn on the fireplace mantel in our bedroom, where it has ever since remained.

Some will say, "She was only a dog."

Yes, she was a dog, but not only a dog. I am a man, but not only a man. Sentiment is not sentimentality, common sense is not common ignorance, and intuition is not superstition. Living with a recognition of the spiritual dimension of the world not only ensures a happier life but also a more honest intellectual life than if we allow no room for wonder and refuse to acknowledge the mystery of existence.

NEVER IN MY career had I suffered writer's block until we lost Trixie. I sat at the keyboard day after day, in the middle of *The Darkest Evening of the Year,* a story full of golden retrievers, and could not advance the manuscript by a single word.

An acquaintance, offering condolences for our loss, admitted that she was embarrassed because she had grieved more for a dog of her own than for family and friends she lost to death. I told her that she had nothing about which to be embarrassed. No matter how close we are to another person, few human relationships are as free from strife, disagreement, and frustration as is the relationship you have with a good dog. Few human beings give of themselves to another as a dog gives of itself. I also suspect that we cherish dogs because their unblemished souls make us wish—consciously or unconsciously—that we were as innocent as they are, and make us yearn for a place where innocence is universal and where the meanness, the betrayals, and the cruelties of this world are unknown.

Saturday afternoon, at the end of the third week of my writer's block, as two o'clock approached, neither Gerda nor I could bear to be apart or to engage in any mundane task. As we'd done the previous two Saturdays, during the hour that Trixie had passed, we walked together, hand in hand, around these two and a half acres that our girl loved, visiting her favorite places. Three weeks to the minute after Trixie died, as we were walking the larger lawn, a brilliant golden butterfly swooped down from a pepper tree. This was no butterfly like any we had seen before; nor have we seen it since. Big, bigger than my hand when I spread my fingers, it was bright gold, not yellow. The butterfly flew around our heads three or four times, brushing our faces, our hair, as no butterfly had ever done before. Swooping back up past the pepper tree, it vanished into the sky. Gerda, who is the most level-headed person I have ever known, said at once, "Was that Trixie?" and without hesitation, I said, "Yeah. It was." We didn't say another word about the experience until later, near bedtime, when we discussed the incredible thickness of the butterfly's wings, which were too thick to be aerodynamic. Gerda remembered them as being "almost edged in a neon rope," and to me, they had appeared to be like stained glass with a leaded edge.

No landscaper who works here has ever before or since seen such a butterfly, nor have we. It danced about our heads at the very minute Trixie had died three weeks earlier. Skeptics will wince, but I will always believe our girl wanted us to know that the intensity of our grief wasn't appropriate, that she was safe and happy. After sharing this story on my Web site, I received hundreds of letters from readers who, after losing beloved dogs, experienced uncanny events that were quite different from ours but that seemed to be intended to tell them that the spirits of their dogs lived on.

FOR EIGHT MONTHS after losing our girl, we could not find the courage to have another dog. Finally, I told Linda

Valliant, the current director of CCI's Southwest Chapter, that we would be ready in two months if they had a release dog that needed a home. Once you have had a wonderful dog, a life without one is a life diminished.

In May 2008, more than ten months after Trixie left us, Linda brought another female golden retriever to us. Her name then was Arianna; her name now is Anna Koontz. Linda didn't know it at the time, but when a few weeks later she gathered the adoption papers on Anna, she discovered that our new girl is the great-niece of our Trixie. Anna's personality is different from Trixie's, but the wonder is the same.

After Trixie's death, Judi Pierson, formerly of CCI, told me that the way by which the magical girl had come to us seemed to have the kiss of destiny to it. When I told Judi, in 1998, that we were at last ready to accept a release dog, she had said there were a number of mooshy ones available. She was going on a two-week vacation and would have our dog for us the day after she returned.

As she left on her vacation, she tasked others with reviewing all the available dogs and selecting from them the best of the lot. In mid-vacation, she learned that a strange thing had happened. Most often, if there are numerous release dogs available at the same time, finding the right homes for them in the CCI family can take a couple months or longer. In this instance, all dogs were placed almost within a weekend, and none remained available.

Having promised us a dog, Judi cut short her vacation,

without telling us, and set out to comb through the organization in search of an animal that might have been overlooked. She discovered that Trixie was never certified for release and was still recuperating after she should have healed. Julia Shular, with whom Trixie was then living, had been considering using her as therapy dog in visits to hospitals and nursing homes.

If all the available dogs had not abruptly been placed in record time, if Judi had simply asked us to wait another couple of months instead of tracking down Trixie, we would have received another dog. That would have been wonderful, too, but it would not have been the same, and another dog might not have wrought in us the changes that Trixie effected.

Trixie was our destiny. And if we had asked for another dog sooner or delayed another month, we would not have received Anna, Trixie's great-niece. Do you detect some wonder and mystery in that? We do.

THIS WORLD IS infinitely layered and mysterious. Every day of our lives, we see far more than we can comprehend, and because the failure to comprehend disquiets us, we lie to ourselves about what we see. We want a simple world, but we live in one that is magnificently complex. Rather than acknowledge the exquisite roundness of creation, we take it in thin slices, and we view each slice through tinted, distorting lenses that further diminish its beauty and obscure truths that await recognition. Complexity implies meaning, and we are afraid of meaning.

The life of a seamstress is no smaller than the life of a queen, the life of a child with Down syndrome no less filled with promise than the life of a philosopher, because the only significant measure of your life is the positive effect you have on others, either by conscious acts of will or by unconscious example. Every smallest act of kindness—even just words of hope when they are needed, the remembrance of a birthday, the compliment that engenders a smile—has the potential to change the recipient's life.

If by the example of her joy and innocence, a dog can greatly change two lives for the better, then no life is little, and every life is big. The mystery of life is the source of its wonder, and the wonder of life is what makes it so worth living.

ON THE IMPORTANCE of the human-dog bond and on the reason why we give our hearts to them knowing what is to come, a character in my novel *The Darkest Evening of the Year* says this:

"Dogs' lives are short, too short, but you know that going in. You know the pain is coming, you're going to lose a dog, and there's going to be great anguish, so you live fully in the moment with her, never fail to share her joy or delight in her innocence, because you can't support the illusion that a dog can be your lifelong companion. There's such beauty in the hard honesty of that, in accepting and giving love while always aware it comes with an unbearable price. Maybe loving dogs is a way we do penance for all the other illusions we allow ourselves and for the mistakes we make because of those illusions."

everafter . . .

FOLLOWING TRIXIE'S PASSING, I asked Linda Valliant if CCI would consider doing Gerda and me a great favor. I hoped they might add Trixie's name to the monument sign at the entrance to the Southwest Chapter's Oceanside campus. This dog, after all, inspired in Gerda and me greater giving than we had done before, and Trixie's writing career pays catastrophic medical bills for the dogs of people with disabilities. The sign now includes her name, and each time I see it, I see the proof that her little life, like every life, changed the lives of others, and I take heart that I will meet her again in a place of wonder, at the center of the mystery around which our existence eternally revolves.